WORKING WOMEN

—A Psychological Perspective

WORKING WOMEN

—A Psychological Perspective

Sapna Sachdeva Nair
Sunita Malhotra

Commonwealth

Working Women—A Psychological Perspective

First Published, 2006

ISBN 81-311-0060-X

Published by:
Ajay Verma
For Commonwealth Publishers
4831/24, Prahlad Street,
Ansari Road, Darya Ganj,
New Delhi - 110002
Phones : 23272541, 23257835
Fax : 91-011-23257835
e-mail-campusbooks@hotmail.com

Typesetting by:
Stylish Laser Typesetter
Delhi - 110053

Printed at:
Roshan Offset Printers
Delhi-110053

FOREWORD

Having a formal work apart from the unpaid household work has become a virtual necessity for women, no matter to which class they belong. It has become essential for their self-respect, autonomy and empowerment. Mahatma Gandhi said, *"Woman is the companion of man, gifted with equal capacities, she has the right to participate in the minutest details of the activities of man, and she has the right of freedom and liberty as he. She is entitled to a supreme place in her own place of activity as man is."* The rapidly increasing number of women in the workforce has given rise to a surge of research aimed at measuring; as they many of them are combining job and family responsibilities. This duplicity of responsibility affects women's lives. The impact of the managing work and family roles simultaneously, affects the Quality of Life of women both positively and negatively. The underlying assumption is that the roles of wife and mother are "natural" roles and are therefore performed without undue stress. In contrast, role of employee is seen as "unnatural" and therefore considered highly demanding. These beliefs foster concern about whether women can handle the demands of multiple roles without serious psychological consequences.

Research on women's roles has centered around two competing ideas. One idea refers to the role enhancement theory, which argues that employment provides psychological and social benefits to women, through increased contact and social interaction with other adults, and increased sense of self-esteem and mastery of a job or skill. On the other hand, the role strain theory proposes that because each person has limited time and energy, women with multiple roles often experience role conflict, which results in harmful effects on their mental and physical health. The authors of the present book, Dr. Sapna Sachdeva Nair and Prof. Sunita Malhotra share some research findings to unveil the complex relationship between multiple social roles and women's psychological health. This book makes a critical contribution by presenting a rich body of data on the women involved in three different professions and at three different levels of social roles (unmarried, married, and married with children) and their consequential psychological effects. Such an assessment is especially important at this particular juncture when demographic trends suggest that the number of employed women is increasing and that the paid employment will be a central component in most women's life experiences. The findings of the present research have long-term effect in the betterment of women's life. Combining home front and work front can be achieved in a satisfying way only if family support in sharing chores is enhanced. Somewhere we have to gender sensitize men so that they can become more helpful husbands and companion.

Prof. Dr. Vidhu Mohan
Consultant
Former Prof. & Chairman
Psychology Dept.
Punjab University
Chandigarh

PREFACE

With the dawn of new millennium, the world today is facing an agonizing array of choices and challenges. We stand poised between a collapsing past and an uncertain future. Both quantitative as well as qualitative changes can be witnessed—quantitative in terms of economic growth and technological changes and qualitative in terms of new paradigm of a society governed by altogether different set of values and ethos. It rings us to the special role; the women are expected to play in this century. In the words of Nancy Smith "... *for every woman who is denied meaningful employment and equal pay, there is a man who must bear full financial responsibility for another human being.... For every woman who takes a step towards her own liberalization, there is a man who finds that the way to freedom has been made a little easier.*"

Indian society is extremely complex, and has remained largely agrarian and traditional, despite decades of modernization efforts since its independence. The present social structure, however reflects changes that have come up through changing frame of time. A major breakthrough at this juncture is the growing education and economic independence among the women. The economic pressures of inflation, influence of the women's movement and the psychological need to develop one's 'self identity' are encouraging the women to take a more active role outside the home to pursue full time careers. This shift, from private to the public domain, and the accompanying economic independence, would lead us to believe that women have finally been liberated from the shackles of patriarchal norms. However, a closer look into the scenario, makes us realize that this picture is far from reality.

Under the pressures of economic crisis most of the middle class families expect their women to contribute to the maintenance of the family. In this way the pursuit of a profession by a women acquires a *'de facto'* legitimacy, which results from a situation of economic necessity but which has not yet led to far reaching ideological and structural changes. This situation is therefore particularly precarious for working women : they must work, but at the same time, they must also conform to an image of womanhood. Women still hold the major responsibility of home and child care while contributing to the paid work. This may be due to the internalization of role responsibilities inculcated through socialization and also due to the available role models.

Fulfilling their economic needs, employment has made women independent with an identifiable social status. At the same time, they appear to be juggling in two main domains of life – work and family, so much so that the issues pertaining to women have become of social and political relevance in India. This fast growing segment of Indian population needs special focus primarily because our society has long way to go before it catches with women's employment trends. Thus, in this context, with the changing social texture of India, the present book is targeted at working women with an attempt to study the psychological consequences as a result of juggling multiple social roles.

The authors are grateful to the women who participated in the study and also to the Department of Psychology, M.D. University, Rohtak for their co-operation. On personal note we are thankful to our families for their constant encouragement and support. Above all, we bow and thank the almighty for showering his blessings and giving us strength to undertake this endeavour successfully.

Sapna Sachdeva Nair

Sunita Malhotra

CONTENTS

1 INTRODUCTION

Whether out of convenience, conviction or tradition, Indian society over the centuries has been "unfair" to the fair sex. Woman has not been allowed to develop self confidence and it is so because before marriage the fair sex is under the thumb of patriarch, and after wedding in awe of her husband and father-in-law. Position of women has undergone a lot of changes from the pre-vedic to the modern times. There has been in fact two phases in the life of women–period of subjection and the period of liberalization. While the former stretched for a longer period, the latter has just begun. For centuries, the women have been deliberately deprived of all the opportunities for growth in the name of religion and ancient socio-cultural practices. At personal-social level, women were victims of widespread illiteracy, feeble health and segregation. At the economic-structural plane, they were prey to economic dependence, absence of career and mobility and non-recognition of their economic contribution. At the socio-political plane, women suffered from denial of freedom even in their home, repression as well as prejudice everywhere.

From time immemorial, the role of man has always been regarded as that of a "Provider" in the social unit of home whereas females were taught to regard marriage as the only thing needful *i.e.,* the only avenue of distinction. Therefore, the women had been directing all their energies in adopting or developing the qualities which were most liked by their spouses and downplaying their intelligence, independence and assertiveness.

Lately the process of urbanization and secularization have speeded up the modernization process and has brought about politico-economic, socio-psychological and cultural changes in life patterns and attitudes of people in our county. The profound social changes which have been witnessed in recent years have affected women much more than men.

"*Adam for field, Eve for hearth*" is no longer relevant. Ambition in the coca-colonised India is scaling new highs, and caught in its vortex are a hitherto content bunch : Well heeled women for whom money matters does not matter. They are no longer happy only being wives of well-placed husbands. But unaccustomed to the bump and grind of aspirational living, these women are falling prey to that new age affliction-depression.

In fact, while social scientists report a change in the aspirational levels among home makers, medical practitioners claim that this is leading to a rise in the incidence of depression. In words of a wife of well placed executive, "I believe well placed husbands are part of the marriage package. ...But as an individual, I aspire to break the day-to-day ties and do what I want to do with myself. But I am not able to do so." Whereas a leading female bureaucrat states that, "Although the aspiration level among women is high because of the opportunities offered by liberalization only a few get any recognition. Society only grants certain freedom to women, but there is more women can do. Hence, there is always a sense of suppression which haunts women" (Chaudhury, 2000).

Women in lower strata of society have been working since long for wages in factories or as unskilled labourers and on construction sites. It was only women of middle or upper classes who were confined at homes and taking up jobs was considered derogatory for them. With the advancement of female education and more liberty for rights and privileges women's attitude towards their stereotyped role is changing and their participation in the workforce is increasing day by day. "Feminization of Employment" due to the increasing labour force participation of women is universally agreed upon as the most significant transformations of the social structure in past decades. By coming out of their homes in gainful employment, women have broken the traditional notion that working outside is derogatory to them or that only under gross economic necessity they can work outside homes. Now it common to see women asserting their presence in all spheres-education, administration, business, medicine, politics, etc.

Besides moving up in the occupational hierarchy and assuming jobs with higher status, increasing number of women are entering non-traditional jobs. Irrespective of the profession, women have to play more than one role. As Shakespeare puts it : *"All the world's a stage and all the men and women merely players. They have their exits and their entrances, and one man in his time plays many parts."* The lasting impression that we make depend to a great extent on the consistency of the parts that we play in theatre of life. But the traits we attribute to people are often merely parts of roles that they play in life. A social role is more or less stereotyped set of responses that one makes to related or similar situations. Some roles (such as being male or female) are basic to one's repertory all through life. Other roles are "bit parts" or "walkons" that one often discards as one matures.

Roles, therefore, are "scripts" for the enactment of particular positions and consist of the expectations for behaviour characteristic of a recognized set of persons in a specific social position or status. The social positions that the individual holds and enacts partially compose the "self". Self can be conceptualized as a set of social identities, where identities refer to positional designations assigned by others and accepted by the individual himself *e.g.* spouse, parent, employee, etc. Role identities not only can help define who one is but also suggest how one ought to behave. In short, from this perspective one's sense of self as meaningful, purposeful entity is derived in part from the social roles one accepts and enacts.

Roles may be learned through a role episode as shown in Fig. 1.1. Group members have expectations about performance, which they communicate either formally or by having the role occupant observe others in similar roles. In stage 3, the role occupant behaves as he or she believes is appropriate. If the behaviour (stage 4) differs widely from the group's expectations (stage 1), the occupant gets feedback from the group regarding

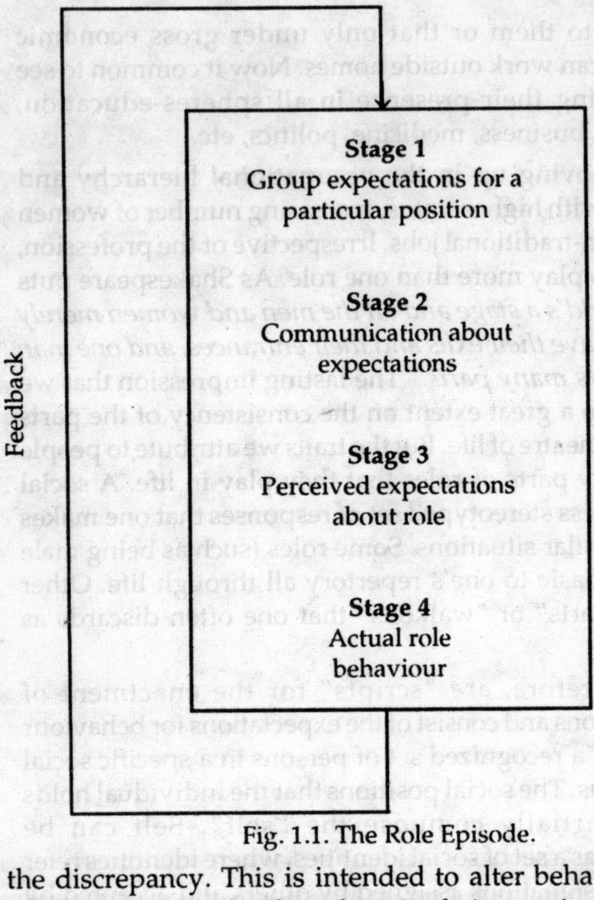

Fig. 1.1. The Role Episode.

the discrepancy. This is intended to alter behaviour towards group expectations. The role episode is ongoing. Expectations may change over time, as might the person's behaviour.

There may be two types of roles-ascribed and achieved roles (Linton, 1936). Ascribed roles are the ones which are assigned to the person without reference to innate differences or abilities *i.e.,* they are thrust upon them without any effort or desire on their part *e.g.* man or woman. Whereas, achieved roles are not assigned by birth, rather they are left open to be filled through competition and individual effort (occupational role behaviours such as teacher). Linton (1936) believed that some roles may limit the extent of a person's development just as the ascribed role such as "women" is a pattern for consistent behaviour, and it does limit the development by not allowing number of achieved roles for *e.g.* earlier women were excluded from law and medical schools. Another classification of roles has been proposed by Banton (1965) which considers the people to possess three types of roles—Basic, General and Independent. He constructed a scale that could measure the extent to which particular roles could be played independently by others.

Basic Roles	General Roles	Independent Roles
Sex roles Religion Skin colour	Occupation	Leisure roles (Cricketer, tennis player)

He further equated basic and ascribed roles. The basic roles such as sex, religion, skin colour or caste are assigned without reference to innate differences or abilities and cannot be differentiated for the reason of not allowing the people to play them independently of others. These roles have the ability to limit the extent or occupational achievement or the scope and type of leisure roles.

Role theory assumes that people behave according to the roles assigned to them, fulfilling the normative demands associated with their position in the social hierarchies. Taken to an extreme, this theory perceives people as no more than their roles.

For the sociologist, to be human is to be socialized. To be socialized is to be roles. To be human, therefore, is to be roles (*Mac Kay, 1973*).

An individual's role repertoire is determined by his or her status in some social system or hierarchy of inter-related statuses. These statuses often specify complementary patterns of rights and obligations. While social statuses are occupied, roles are played therefore, roles are the dynamic aspect of status. The status of being married, for instance, can include the roles of spouse, parent and in-law. These roles are dynamically related. One cannot play the role of parent without someone playing the role of a child.

This theory bridges the gap between the micro-social level (individuals and small groups) and macro-social level of analysis (large groups, institutes and societies) in two ways—Roles are enacted by individual but the society determines the existing position underlying them; Role transcends the individuals.

Biddle and Thomas (1966) formulated a role theory which consisted of four basic terms—Actor, Role, Personality, Role conflict.

The "actor" is a person who is currently behaving in a given role in relation with an alter, the target or others. The alter is an individual who bears relationship to the actor and his role. A "role" has been defined in many ways depending on the investigators' school of thought as, "an internally consistent series of conditioned responses by one member of a serial situation which represents the stimulus pattern for a similarly, internally consistent series of conditioned responses of others in that situation (Cottrell, 1942); as, "a pattern or type of social behaviour which seems situationally appropriate to him in terms of the demands and expectations of those in his group (Seargent, 1975); as, "the expectations that persons hold in common towards any person who falls in a particular category by virtue of his position in the social system. (Secord and Backman, 1964).

Although an actor is expected to perform his role according to role prescription but he may not conform to the expectations all the time because role performance is also influenced by the expectations from self. Sometimes actor's personal characteristics such as needs, attitudes, ability and self concept interferes with the smooth and almost automatic quality of interaction between persons. The role theory holds that an actor's behaviour may be best understood as a function of role and "personality".

Sometimes certain situations are so structured that an actor is required to fill simultaneously two or more roles that present contradictory, or even mutually exclusive expectations. The actor cannot realistically conform to these expectations and this leads to role conflict. That is what generally happens when a woman has to perform the roles of housewife and an employee simultaneously. It is a fact that all women work. But their work goes unrecognized because they do a variety of jobs daily which does not fit into any specific "occupation". Most of them are involved in arduous household work. The so-called housewife is already doing a single shift. If woman also works outside home, she is consistently working double shift.

Working women have a whole new set of problems, involving both family and professional lives. Since, the working women go beyond their boundary lines of their homes, they seem to be deviating from their traditional role of wives. Such things may affect both—the role of women as well as the interpersonal relations with their husbands. Having different social roles (single/daughter, wife, mother and so on) might interact with their role of wage earner to produce differential psychological effect. Like, for the unmarried who take up professional occupations do not involve much of a problems as they do not have any other major responsibility. But for married working women, the picture is quite different as they have to enter into the area of role conflict between various roles of women as wife, mother and an earner. While for men, family connotes provisions of comfort and support, for working women it means two sets of overlapping responsibilities. Therefore, the role of family caretaker in addition to their professional role seems to be one of the major source of stress that working women have to face.

Kahn *et al.* (1964) was the earliest to draw attention to the organizational stress in general and role stress in particular. Role as the position occupied by a person and as defined by the expectations of significant persons, including role occupant, indicate that there are inherent problems in performance of a role and therefore, the stress is inevitable (Pareek, 1976).

Kahn and Quinn (1970) classified role stress under three main headings :

(i) Expectation generated stress, in which they included role ambiguity and role conflict.

(ii) Expectation resource discrepancies in which they included role overload, responsibility-authority dilemma.

(iii) Role and personality.

Role ambiguity occurs when there is unclearity regarding a role or when person cannot discover the dimensions of his role expectations. There are generally five sources of ambiguity-people are confused about role expectations, the boundaries of acceptable and unacceptable behaviour, the situation in which the role applies, whether behaviour is obligatory or optional, and which of the two or more expectations should be given priority (Secord and Backman, 1974). Ambiguity provides enough scope for variations in work as role performance by individuals, thereby increasing opportunities for conflict. The Fig. 1.2 illustrates how role conflict develop from out of divergent role expectations.

When an individual's role demands more time and effort than the individual has for them, role overload occurs. There may be two types of overload-qualitative and quantitative overload (Marshall and Cooper, 1979). While quantitative refers to having "too much to do", qualitative refers to the work that is "too difficult".

Moreover, five main role stressors or conflicts in the role space of an individual that have been identified are :

Self-Role Distance—This is the conflict between the self concept and the expectations from the role as perceived by the role occupant.

Intra-Role Conflict—Since the individual learns to develop expectations as a result of his socialization and identification with significant others, it is quite likely that he sees some incompatibility between the two expectations from his own role.

Role Stagnation—Individual grows in the role he occupies

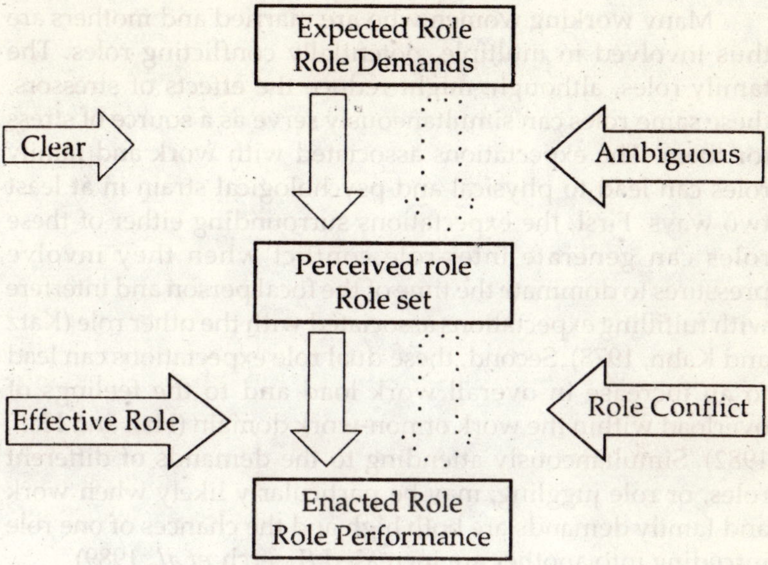

Fig. 1.2. Diagramatic representation of role Ambiguity.

in organization. With the advancement of individual, his role changes and with this change in role, the need for taking his new role becomes crucial. This is the problems of role growth. This becomes an acute problem especially when an individual has occupied a role for a long time, and he enters another role in which he may feel less secure. The new role demands individual to outgrow his previous role and occupy the new role effectively and this produces some stress in the individual.

Role Boundless—An individual feels highly obligated to expectations of significant role senders and sacrifices his own interest, value, comfort, etc. He may be called role bound and may experience conflict between his tendency to live as a person and live as a role.

Inter-Role Distance—An individual occupies more than one role. There may be conflicts between the two roles he occupies. Such conflict are more common in today's modern society when the individual is increasingly occupying multiple roles as in case of women, whose burgeoning participation in workforce may have a knock on effect on their family.

Many working women who are married and mothers are thus involved in multiple, potentially conflicting roles. The family roles, although, might reduce the effects of stressors, these same roles can simultaneously serve as a source of stress for them. The expectations associated with work and family roles can lead to physical and psychological strain in at least two ways. First, the expectations surrounding either of these roles can generate inter-role conflict when they involve pressures to dominate the time of the focal person and interfere with fulfilling expectations associated with the other role (Katz and Kahn, 1978). Second, these dual role expectations can lead to an increase in overall work load and to the feelings of overload within the work or non-work domain (Hall and Hall, 1982). Simultaneously attending to the demands of different roles, or role juggling, may be particularly likely when work and family demands are both high and the chances of one role intruding into another are increased (Loerch *et al.,* 1989).

A key assumption underlies current theories of social roles—that multiple relationships with diverse role partners is a source of psychological stress and social instability. Problems can accumulate across roles, but so can rewards; participation in multiple roles may cancel some of the negative effects generated by a particular role. Had it not been so, we would not have witnessed women as the greatest addition in the workforce. Positive outcomes of role accumulation may be classified into : role privileges, overall status security, resources for status enhancement and role performance, enrichment of personality or ego-gratification.

Each role carries with it certain rights as well as duties. Some of these rights are inherent rights which are built into role. Other rights or emergent rights arise from daily interaction with role partners. Inherent rights serve as inducements for recruitment of roles and as inducements for compliance of role performance. Emergent rights serve the more specialized function of guaranteeing role compliance, especially when the demands of roles are increased. Thus, the allotment of rights seem to be contingent to some degree on the level of obligations and adequacy of performance. As privileges are part and parcel of almost every social role, therefore, greater the number of roles, greater the number of privileges enjoyed by an individual.

Another way in which multiple roles might compensate for role strain is through providing numerous buffers against failure in the instrumental and expressive domains of action. An individual with a wide array of role partners compensate for the failure in any particular social sphere or relationship by falling back on other relationships. These alternative relationships afford compensatory affection, moral support, emergency resources and perhaps even assistance for renewal of effort in the original role.

In addition to the sense of overall status security, role partners afford a variety of incidental emoluments. These are the non-institutionalized by-products of social relationships like recommendations, or connections, gifts of all kinds, etc. While the supply of perquisites may be increased as a result of better role performance, they are made available by virtue of sheer occupancy of a position.

Besides providing privileges, buffers and resources, role accumulation may also enrich the personality: Increased autonomy, tolerance of discrepant viewpoints, flexibility in adjusting to the demands of role partners, reduction in boredom etc. may also enhance one's self-esteem. "Self esteem" refers to the evaluation a person makes and customarily maintains with regard to himself or herself. It expresses an attitude of approval or disapproval (Rosenberg, 1965). As Shibutani (1961) puts it "Each person places some kind of estimate upon himself as an object of value". This evaluative, judgmental, or affective aspect of a person's self conception involves the process commonly known as the self esteem. It may be viewed as attitudes, relation between attitudes and selves, psychological response as well as personality function.

As attitudes, the self esteem is a more or less phenomenal process in which the person perceives characteristics of herself/himself and reacts to those characteristics emotionally or behaviourally. This conception utilizes the idea of attitude in any of its various meanings—cognitions, feelings, beliefs, predispositions to act, etc. Self esteem indicates the extent to which a person believes himself or herself capable, significant, successful and worthy. In short, a person's self esteem is a judgment of worthiness that is expressed by attitudes he or she holds towards self. It is a subjective experience conveyed by verbal reports and other overt expressive behaviour.

Self esteem may also be regarded as a psychological relation between different sets of attitudes. James (1892) emphasized the interconnections among self conceptions, aspirations, social outcomes and the resulting changes in self evaluations. He noted that many desired selves must be put aside, while only certain of the potential selves (characters) that the person might develop actually receive attention and energy. On the basis of this analysis of the self, James formulated what is known as the law of self esteem according to which self esteem is the rations of success and pretensions. It involves two sets of attitudes—how the person actually perceives himself to be with respect to some quality or ability and how he might be or ought to be.

Besides describing self esteem as an attitude, Rosenberg (1965) further explained it as a psychological response. According to him, high self esteem...expresses the feeling that one is good enough. The individual simply feels that he is a person of worth, he respects himself for what he is. Self esteem is not taken as an attitudinal or perceptual processes, but by specifying "what it feels like".

A major exception of the common attitudinal description of self esteem is the filed-theoretical description associated with Ziller (1969) who explained self esteem as a component of the self system which regulates the extent to which the self system is maintained under conditions of strain, such as during the processing of new information concerning the self. High self esteem equals high regulation.

Ziller's self esteem is strikingly similar to the idea of ego strength discussed by Symonds (1951) *i.e.*, "the efficiency of the ego in regulating impulses and mastering the environment," "the capacity to react successfully to environmental stress," and "the degree of rigidity" (structure).

Self esteem is derived from some of the same sources as the self. Significant others provide one component of self esteem, with the most significant other providing the most important impetus into the self esteem. Moreover, social comparisons and self attributions also contribute to self esteem. Level of self esteem is based on the assessment of only those qualities that count. Individuals tend to value those qualities at which they excel. There are four types of selectivity that allows individual to choose judgments they make about themselves. First, behaviour can be interpreted selectively. Most behaviour can be viewed in a positive light. Second, standards can be selectively set. Absolute performance is less important than the relative performance. Most people choose standards of performance that are well within their limitations. Third, people use interpersonal selectivity, *i.e.* they tend to expose themselves to the information consistent with their beliefs and associate with people like them. Fourth, people select their environment. They seek environment in which they will be accepted and situations in which they feel they will excel.

Self esteem has important implications for the behaviour. People who are high in self esteem have more confidence in their opinions, and thus are more likely to influence others and are less likely to be influenced by others. In case of working women the ability to enact multiple roles may contribute to the self esteem because performing different tasks and interacting with more role partners might increase their sense of competence and equip them to deal with wide range of situations. Self esteem, in turn, may be associated with a number of indices of mental health like feelings of vulnerability and submissiveness on negative side and with self acceptance, self respect and satisfaction with life on the positive side.

Closely related to life satisfaction is the concept of "Quality of Life" (QOL). Since everyone irrespective of age, education, occupation, status etc. makes continuous efforts to live happily in life, it becomes all the more important to understand this concept. In a popular sense, quality of life is often associated with positive values such as happiness, wealth, success or even good health. Presently, there is no commonly agreed upon definition of the concept since the quality of life research is relatively new. Most fields use a broad framework, and quality of life is treated as an all inclusive notion of life and living (Szalai, 1980). Many disciplines such as Philosophy, Sociology, Medicine and Behavioural Science have taken interest in quality of life research.

Philosophy—Defining the Good Life

One of the basic concepts of life is survival and phenomenon that enhance or reduce survival are fundamentally the quality of life issues.

Sociology—Being Happy

Social Science approaches 'Quality of Life' by determining human needs and demands. In Sociology, quality of life is defined in terms of non-material values such as social networks or relations to society and nature. Within this framework both the objective conditions and subjective perceptions about the conditions are important.

Medicine—Staying Normal

Medical Science traditionally has been involved in the diagnosis and treatment of disease and the fundamental goal has been the maintenance of physiological life. It was the development of the possibility to sustain life in life threatening conditions such as cancer, that stimulated research into the quality of survival and introduced the concept of quality of life in the medical world.

Behavioural Science—Feeling Well

Quality of Life (QOL) has been used as a description of objectives of life within behavioural science. Good mental health has been defined as having a positive self concept, being active and capable of developing one's own skills, being an integrated person and also to make important decisions and take action without isolation, having a good sense of realty and empathetic skills, and finally create deep and lasting, human relations. World Health Organization (WHO) considers QOL as the individuals' perception of their position in life in the context of the culture and value systems in which they live and in relation to their goals, expectations, standards and concerns. It is a broad ranging concept incorporating in a complex way an individual's physical health, psychological state, level of independence, social relationships, personal beliefs and her/his relationship to salient features of environment. This definition highlights QOL as a subjective self report from the individual which is not based on reports of judgments from others. QOL is also multidimensional, incorporating positive (*e.g.* feeling happy, energetic) as well as negative aspects (*e.g.* sadness, fatigue).

Campbell et al (1970) considered Quality of Life as a composite measure of physical, mental and social well being, happiness and satisfaction involving many life situations, such as health, marriage, family, work, financial situation, educational opportunities, creativity, belongingness and trust in others. Similarly, Cutter (1986) stated that "Quality of Life" is an individual's happiness or satisfaction with life and environment including needs, desires, aspirations, life style, preferences and other tangible and intangible factors which determine overall well being.

A conventional view is that there is a direct positive relationship between Quality of Life and quality of the person. A higher QOL improves quality of human in mutually self reinforcing manner. Deterioration of QOL inevitable leads to deterioration of quality of person which may in turn affect his level of adjustment.

The word 'adjustment' is often used in our daily life and refers to the individuals ability to satisfy the demands of one's surroundings as well as one's own need. Wolman (1973) defined adjustment as :

1. A harmonious relationship with the environment

involving the ability to satisfy most of one's needs and meet most of the demands, both physical and social, that are put upon one.

2. The variation and changes in behaviour that are necessary to satisfy needs and meet demands so that one can establish a harmonious relationship with the environment.

Although person may sometimes face some problems in making these adjustments, they are important to maintain personal as well as social peace and harmony.

Mental health professionals earlier spoke of the "well adjusted personality" as an ideal to emulate. Such an ideal person was stable, dependable, happy, free from anxiety and other problems as possible and able to get along harmoniously with others. Is was assumed that such personal characteristics were equally desirable for everyone and that conventional society was a conductive setting in which to acquire them. Adjustment involved a great deal of social conformity because in order to survive socially, one had to become "normal" like everyone else. But in this world when everything, including the social norms themselves change, it was difficult to explain what exactly is meant by "well adjusted". Therefore, some psychologists have modified the meaning of adjustment to include more of a two-way relationship between individual and his surroundings. As Lazarus (1976) pointed out, "actually adjustment is fitting oneself into given circumstances and changing the circumstances to fit one's needs." Hence, a good adjustment involves more than a passive relationship with one's surroundings. It involves taking initiative, taking risks and learning to make the most of a situation instead of resigning one's self to it. Mental health professionals are also becoming more aware that, in addition to adjusting to one's environment, one must also adjust to oneself, to one's own biological and psychological capabilities. In this sense of term, adjustment refers to internal processes of psychological health, growth and self actualisation.

The millennium started with the celebrations of Women Empowerment Year, therefore, the focal issues related to them can't be ignored. Though there has been plethora of studies concerning women's problems but the challenges, emerging out of the job demands in addition to the family demands and their possible psychological effects seems to be the burning issue of the modern times. How does being employed besides occupying different social roles affect women in personal, emotional as well as social fronts is becoming topic of general interest.

With this background we move to next chapter for reviewing the nature of studies conducted to assess the impact of multiple roles on women's psychological and physical health.

2 WOMEN AND MULTIPLE SOCIAL ROLES : EMPERICAL EVIDENCES IN EASTERN AND WESTERN CONTEXT

Over the past half century, as women's participation in the labour force and career opportunities expanded, researchers turned attention to the effects of fulfilling multiple roles on women's health. This chapter will review the literature examining the impact of multiple roles on women's psychological and physical health. Grounded in the existing literature reviewed, this chapter will conclude with rationale of proposed study and hypotheses describing anticipated outcomes for the study.

Prior to the industrial revolution in the United States, both women and men engaged in the production of goods throughout the agricultural era. Although women focused primarily on the production of domestic items, work and family responsibilities were interwoven for both men and women (Hattery, 2001). At the turn of the 20th century the industrial revolution brought about a distinction between paid and unpaid work as women focused on the private sphere of unpaid labour in the home, and men focused on the public sphere of paid work. Despite this broad distinction, women facing economic constraints were more likely than women of higher income levels to engage in paid work throughout the 20th century (Reskin & Padavic, 1994). Due to a depleted work-force, women's participation in paid labour increased dramatically during World War II. Later in the 1970's and 80's, women's labour force participation increased again as economic growth decreased and social acceptance of women working outside home increased. Today, employment is of great importance, indeed a central prerequisite, for meeting the socially defined needs of people in western society (Nordenmark and Strandh 1999). Winefield *et al.* (2002) described that paid work in western society is highly valued and can dramatically impact on individual identity and status. According to them, not to have paid work is to see oneself as a failure, to have an indeterminate identity and status, to be perceived as carried by the work of others, to be dependent, and to have an uncertain future.

Indian society on the other hand has been extremely complex and its social and economic structures are significantly different from those in western industrial societies. India has remained largely traditional especially with regard to woman's status and roles. By tradition, the role of women in Hindu society has been that of a housewife (gruhini). The traditional role model sees the ideal situation as the one in which husband is the primary bread winner. In words of American Alice 'Elizabeth Bumiller', "*it is a bitter truth and a choiceless reality that Indian women have not yet come out of the shackles of 'womanhood attire' imposed successfully on them by men.*" More and more women may be stepping into work place still the emphasis is on women accommodating to other's needs: Earning a wage is not seen to be of intrinsic value to a woman's life, rather as an exception, a kind of added extra. Some scholars have even compared women to the ethnic minority. Wirth (1938) long back defined a minority as, "a group of people who because of their physical or cultural characteristics are singled out from others in the society in which they live for differential and unequal treatment....". He noted that minorities could be distinguished by the exclusion from full participation in the society, their debarment from certain economic, political and social opportunities, the "restricted scope of their occupational and professional advancement and the general tendency to treat them as members of a category irrespective of their individual merits". On the basis of this criterion set forth by Wirth there seems to be little doubt that women qualify as minority group.

But today, the growth of education by and large, has led to a large number of women in different spheres of life. By gaining employment outside homes, they seeking different identities. In 1930, Coit and Harper identified survival and economic needs as the reasons for women taking up the jobs. Besides these, the non-economic factors like self expression, personal development, emotional and intellectual satisfaction have also been reported to be important for female's participation in labour force (Chakraborty, 1977). Since combining these two roles require not only skill but also physical and psychological acceptance besides some sacrifices and adjustments to the changes brought about by this combination, the primary question investigated throughout the literature on the effects of multiple role occupancy is whether multiple role involvement is beneficial; and/or detrimental to the person fulfilling multiple roles. Combining these two roles require not only skill but also physical and psychological acceptance besides some sacrifices and adjustments to the changes brought about by this combination. Studies in this area have shown that the effect of employment may vary according to job characteristics as well as women's characteristics.

The job characteristics includes social support at work, occupational category and specific job characteristics. Holahan and Moos (1981) found lack of support at work to be associated with depression. No difference was found in the mortality among women in three categories of employment : professional and managerial, clerical, sales and blue collar (House *et al.*, 1986). On the contrary, Dentre *et al.* (1987) reported lower mortality for physicians and high level managers and professionals relative to the general population. LaCroix and Haynes (1987) indicated that high job demands in combination with lack of clarity of expectations led to an increased risk of Coronary Heart Disease (CHD).

Besides, job characteristics, women's attitude towards employment, their marital status and maternal status may also effect their mental health. Waldron and Herold (1986) suggested that for married women, labour force participation had beneficial influence on self reported general health only among those with favourable attitude towards employment. Similar results have been reported by Parry (1987) who found the association between employment and good health to be stronger for women who preferred employment to being a home maker.

More beneficial effects of labour force participation on self reported general health have been shown for unmarried women than married women by Waldron and Jacobs (1989). If one disadvantage of employment is multiple role strain (Goode, 1960), then one might expect employment to have a more negative effect on the health of mothers when compared to non-mothers.

Women, Multiple Roles, Role Conflict

The first theory regarding human energy and multiple roles, entitled the scarcity hypothesis, was developed by Goode (1960). This hypothesis stipulated that human beings have a limited amount of energy to expend, and the role strain may occur as an individual accumulates more roles and responsibilities. The accumulation of life roles that exceeds an individual's personal resources was assumed to lead conflicting obligations and exhaustion. Applied to women, this theory extended by Coser (1974) and Slater (1963) suggested that women who occupy multiple roles experience greater distress than women who occupy fewer life roles. Getzels and Guba (1954) found that conflict may accentuate when the relative incompatibility of expectation is involved and the rigour with which these expectations are defined. Thus, out of the three roles of wife, mother and employee, a woman occupying roles of wife and employee will experience more conflict than a women occupying role of wife and mother because of the greater incompatibility between the roles. Moreover, her conflict would be all the more intense if her employer, her husband as well as family members held unreasonable expectations from her.

Bardwick (1971); Holahan and Gilbert (1979) also reported that women who assumed home roles (*e.g.* wife, mother and home maker) and non-home roles (*e.g.* employee) frequently experienced conflict between competing role demands. Conflicts were considered likely when women perceived their home and career roles as highly desirable but mutually exclusive goals. The role in which three is high commitment to other people is subject to considerable internal conflict (Farmer, 1971).

Coser and Rokoff (1977) found that married working

partners, who had to attend to their job related matters while keeping the family running smoothly, might well experience stress from simultaneous handling of several conflicting roles—that of a career person, spouse, parents, etc. Such stresses are usually consciously experienced outside the work place and may be felt more by wives than by husbands, since quite often, it is the women who devote more time and energy to run the house and attending family and social obligations. Similarly, Hall (1972) reported higher inter-role conflict for women than for men because women are more likely to process work and family roles simultaneously rather than sequentially. Simultaneous role demands require setting priorities while sequential role demands set their own priority.

According to Bhatty and Bhatty (1971) number and age of children are directly related to role conflict in working women because mother's personal attention is most essential to children when they are small. Fewer children means less work and subsequently less role conflict among working mothers (Singh, 1972).

Grace (1972) claimed that there may be functional as well as dysfunctional effect of certain types of role conflict. Conflicts can be functional to the individual, the organization or the society, acting as a stimulus to the analysis of problems and a motive force behind porgrammes of changes and reform. Role conflict can also be disruptive and tension inducing with adverse effects both for the role occupants and the organizations of which he/she is a member (Parson, 1951). Kahn *et al.,* in 1964 reported that the consequences of role conflict may be reduction of commitment or abandonment of certain objectives by the individual (role retreatism), reduced satisfaction with a role in a particular situation (job dissatisfaction or increased personal strain and anxiety).

For women, the gratifications associated with the family roles, particularly the role of wife and mother have been emphasized over the costs. The concept of role overload and role conflict are primarily used to analyse the complications that employment causes for married women, especially mothers. Role conflict and role overload inherent in women's family roles have been ignored. The assumption has been that the role of mother, wife, and homemaker fit together easily, at least more easily than any of these roles does with that of paid worker. (Oakley, 1974).

Kapur (1974) indicated that women who choose to combine marriage with career face almost a situation of normlessness and they hardly know how to apportion time and resources between these two major responsibilities. This makes them experience great conflict, tension and strain. Nurses are particularly vulnerable to inter-role conflict between family and work as well as overload from both sets of responsibilities as both marital role and occupational role are greedy in demanding time, energy and commitment (Coser, 1974). On the contrary, Pearlin (1975) noted that even the non-employed married women experienced stress which he believed is often due to 'severe demands in their employment inside the home'. Gove and Geerken (1977) also found that among married women, the non-employed reported more demands on them than the employed and hence showed more symptoms of psychiatric symptomatology.

According to Pleck (1977) one source of inter-role conflict in working women is the extent to which family roles intrudes into the work role and vice-versa. Chakraborty (1977) suggested various sources of potentiality for the conflict, namely, diffused nature of role, working women's concern with status (Rani, 1976; Orden and Bradburn, 1968), the effectivity and moral orientation of the role and conflict due to incompatible expectations (Gordon and Hall, 1974). Holahan and Gilbert (1979) appraised that, "one would anticipate that women in dual carreer marriage are experiencing higher role conflict than their spouses since they are now actively involved in adding a role (*i.e.* professionals) which may require attitude and behaviour that are inconsistent with those of their more traditional roles (*i.e.* spouse and parent)." Self role (personal desires, ambitions) and time factor are other two sources or role conflict which have been identified by Sinha in 1981.

Traditionally, married woman is responsible for larger share of housework. This also applies to working married women. Different activities attached to different roles require definite amount of time in a day. Limitation of time always produce role conflict among working women (Dahlstrom, 1967).

Rapoport and Rapoport (1978) observed that the extent of time and ego involvement in work and family roles may differ substantially for husbands and wives. The greater salience man places on his work, the greater will be their preoccupation with work and hence the less frequent their participation in family roles. This is likely to enforce family involvement on women, which may prevent them from investing more of their time and themselves in work, as they attempt to fulfil several roles simultaneously. Paterson (1978) confirmed that the job taking by women created more conflicting situations for them due to dual role played and inability to tolerate the whole burden. Gutek *et al.* (1981) also found that the inter-role conflict is likely to increase as the demands of either the work role or family role increases. Similarly, inter-role conflict can increase as one's obligations to the family expand through marriage and the arrival of children. Keith and Schafer (1980) reported duty hours to be an important variable in context of role conflict. With regard to the symptoms of stress, working women reported more daily stress than the housewives (Haynes and Feinleib, 1980). Bohen and Long (1981) found responsibilities of child rearing and household chores to be a major source of work-family conflict in women. Similar results have been reported by Haw in 1982 but, Sen (1981) found unmarried women to be more stressed when compared to married women.

Riesch (1984); Sound and Ostwald (1985) pointed out the difficulties working women have to face in managing different roles. Besides dealing with the household responsibilities they also have to deal with the stresses associated with their occupational role. Barnett and Baruch (1985) found that role conflict and levels of overload were significantly associated with occupying the role of mother but were not significantly associated with occupying the role of paid worker or wife.

However, Greenhaus and Beutell (1985) reported that work family conflict resulted from incompatible demands arising simultaneously from family and work roles. They identified three types of work family conflict : *(a)* time based, *(b)* strain based and *(c)* behaviour based. Kopelman *et al.* (1983) found that intrusion by family into work has the potential to create conflict in women as the socially prescribed sex-role norm of women as primary caretakers of family may conflict with job norms. Verbrugge (1986) postulated 'overload' to be a mediator having important links between employment and negative health consequences.

Both working women and housewives have been reported to experience stress due to role versus reward character of their lives by Aneshensel (1986). He maintained that in both cases, women who received affilication for who they are, and what they do, experienced less psychological strain than women who did not receive support. However, Baruch *et al.* (1987) suggested the unemployed women to experience greater stress than employed women. Mothers feel responsible for the continuing success and happiness of their children and are often blamed when anything goes wrong in their children's lives.

Burke and Greenglass (1987) found that work-family conflict may arise because of "intra role" or "inter role" conflict. Voydonoff (1988) called inter-role conflict as strain in working women due to the demands of work-family customs and traditions, often viewed as incompatible. Consequently working wives engage in a "zero sum" activity, *i.e.* more they devote themselves to one sphere, the less they have for the other.

Everly (1989); Repetti *et al.* (1989) reported that stress may be created by various types of overload like multiple tasks, time demands, etc.

Aleshina and Lektorskaya (1989) studied the psychological factors determining the way in which professional family roles are combined and the degree of success in resolving role conflict. Emmons *et al.* (1990) reported that the stress of managing multiple roles is greatest and the psychological benefits least when work and family responsibilities are both heavy. In particular, mothers entering the work force continue to bear a disproportionate share of household and child care responsibilities (Hochschild, 1989; Lewis and Copper, 1988). As a result, home and work responsibilities may frequently be placed in opposition or conflict to one another. Similarly, dissatisfaction with child care arrangement has been linked with role strain in working women by VanMeter and Agronow (1982).

Ilyas (1990) examined the joint linear influence of several variables on the Perceived Role Conflict (PRC) of women. These variables included wife's age, her income, her time for household chores and outside job, her Female Role Perception (FRP), husband's income, his time for household work and outside job, total number of children, child density, age of youngest child and age of oldest unmarried girl. Regression analysis indicated that 27.12% of variance of PRC was explained by all the independent variables operating jointly. However, FRP alone explained 20.61% variance of PRC.

Sex differences have been observed in the work-family conflict. Wortman *et al.* (1991) reported that combining profession with parental role generates more stress in women compared to men. Earlier, Russo in 1976 also found professional women experiencing more conflict than men due to difficulty in managing the work family interface. Similarly, Cooper and Marshal (1976) considered work to be a significant source of stress especially for women, which may be tied to serious consequences in regard to their mental and physical ill health.

Greenglass (1991) investigated relationship between Type A behaviour, career aspirations and role conflict in faculty women and found Type A scores to be positively and significantly correlated with role conflict. The higher the Type A, the higher the role conflict in areas involving work and familial areas.

200 married professional women aged (23-47 years) with at least 1 child aged 1 to 6 years living at home were surveyed by Reifman *et al.* (1991) to investigate types of occupational and role conflict stresses associated with physical and

depressive symptoms. Six stress indices predicted physical and depressive symptoms. These stresses reflected perceptions of lack of authority and influence on the job, a heavy work load, sex discrimination, work imposing on relaxation, family imposing on relaxation, and overall suffering from role conflict.

Frone *et al.* (1992) reported combination of career and family roles to be often associated with conflict, overload and stress. The impact of five antecedent sets of work and family domain variables on three types of work family conflict (job spouse, job parent and job homemaker) have been examined by Aryee (1992). The results indicated married professional women to experience moderate amounts of each type of work-family conflict. Role stressors explained most of the variance in job-spouse and job-homemaker conflict, while task characteristics explained the most variance in job parent conflict.

While earlier studies treated work-family conflict as global, bidirectional construct, the more recent work has suggested that family to work conflict and work to family conflict effects are related but distinct forms of inter role conflict (O' Driscoll *et al.* 1992). Three 3 competiting views on the processes of role interaction between work and family have emerged. These include *(a)* spill over, in which attitudes and behaviour are posited to carry over from one role to another (Leiter and Durup, 1996); *(b)* compensation, in which roles are often thought to be interrelated in a counterbalancing manner (Greenglass and Burke, 1988); and *(c)* segmentation, in which it is assumed that one can compartmentalize competing role demands (Lambert, 1990). Cooke and Rousseau (1984) investigated contradictory models of the effects of family roles and work role expectations on strain and family roles to be related to strain. Family roles interacted with work role expectations so that the relation between those expectation and work overload was progressively greater for single teachers, those who were married and those who had children; they were indirectly related to strain through their relation to inter-role conflict.

Barker (1993) conducted a survey of 315 predominantly white women working Part Time (PT) or Full Time (FT) in male dominated professions (law, executives), female dominated profession (nursing, elementary education) and non-professional jobs (clerical, retail sales). PT working women reported greater happiness at home and work, greater satisfaction and personal satisfaction with work compared with FT working women. However, they did not report lower role conflict and role overload.

In 1993, Rankin studies women employed and enacting multiple roles. 118 employed mothers (aged 23-43 years) of pre-school children were interviewed. Out of 100 subjects (Ss) who described how stressful their lives were, 62% reported a high level of stress, with 25% indicating "very stressful". The number of stressors indicated by Ss reflected the many roles they fulfilled.

Caltabiano and Caltabiano (1994) addressed the theoretical Type E construct proposed by Braiker in 1986 as an explanation for multiple role stress by documenting the prevalence of Type E behaviour in career women, by investigating its validity in relation to Type A behaviour, examining the relationship of Type E stress to illness symptoms and studying stress buffering effects of social support. All Ss were involved in multiple roles relating to work, marriage/partnership, and child rearing. The Type E construct was found to be independent of Type A construct. Type E personality was found to be strongly related to illness symptoms, the cognitive aspect of the syndrome being even better predictor of symptoms than Type E behaviours.

In the study on multiplicity role in working women, Napholz (1995) found that Ss whose work had first or equal priority had significantly higher role conflict scores than Ss who put their relationships first.

Moore *et al.* (1995) examined work-family role conflict among Jewish women, 72 who were employed in a female typed profession (secondary school teacher) and 40 who were employed in a male typed occupation (university professors). Women in a male type occupation spend less time on family and domestic roles and increased their hours of work which consequently decreased their burden at home. Because the burden at home contributes more to role conflict than the burden at work, women in male typed occupations reported less role than did women in typically female occupations.

Luecken *et al.* (1997) evaluated the biological and psychological effects of role overload by examining the effects of marital status and parental status (defined as having children at home) on daily excretion of urinary catecholamines and cortisol in employed women. These findings indicated that working women with children at home, independent of marital status, social support, excreted greater amounts of cortisol and experience higher levels of home strain than those without children at home.

Pareek and Mehta (1997) in their study compared three group of working women, *i.e.* gazetted officers, bank employees and school teachers on the types of role streses they experienced. The eight categories of role stress measured were Self Role Distance (SRD), Inter-Role Distance (IRD), Role Stagnation (RS), Role Ambiguity (RA), Role Overload (RO), Role Isolation (RI), Role Erosion (RE), and Role Inadequacy (RIn). The results showed school teachers to be lower on all kinds of role stresses in comparison to gazetted officers and bank employees. Mishra *et al.* (1998) traced some of the predictors of work-family conflict among Indian working women with identifying the area where conflict was experienced to a maximum extent. Occupational differences (both type and level) with regard to role conflict were analysed. The results revealed that profession versus parent area exhibited maximum, though moderate conflict. Occupational type did not leave any significant impact on role-conflict whereas clerks were found to experience greater conflict than officer grade employees.

Chattopadhyay and Dasgupta (1999) however concluded that one could be married and play the role of wife, mother, householder and executive effectively and yet experience not more role stress(s) than their single counterparts. More recently, studies have examined individual factors such as role centrality (Martire *et al.,* 2000) and self-determination (Senecal *et al.,* 2001) in relation to women's psychological health and experience of work-family conflict. Overall, these recent studies suggest that individual factors are also important considerations in this area of study.

Women, Multiple Roles, Self Esteem

Contrary to the earlier theoretical formulations (*e.g.* Goode, 1960) which accentuated how involvement in multiple social roles could elicit strain, the Expansion or the Role Accumulation Hypothesis emphasized that multiple roles appear to have a positive and beneficial impact on women's psychological and physical health (Barnett, 1991; Hong & Seltzer, 1995) and can lead to personal growth and development (*e.g.* Sieber, 1974; Marks, 1977). Individuals may profit from enacting multiple roles in terms of more sources of social support, self esteem and financial resources and these benefits outweigh any disadvantages resulting from multiple role juggling (Meon *et al.,* 1992; Waldron and Jacobs, 1989). In its simplest formulation, it proposes an approximately additive, monotonic relationship, with more roles resulting in better health.

According to Glenn (1975) marital roles are important sources of identity for women, so being successfully married should increase woman's self esteem. However, the specific role requirements of marriage also produce stress (Bernard, 1972), thereby reducing women's self esteem. Macke and Bohrnstedt (1979) further pointed out that the relative lack of independent achievement combined with close attention to husband's success may lower the housewife's self esteem. Similarly, Neiva and Gutek (1981); McRae (1982) also reported higher self esteem in women who were in employment.

According to Terborg (1977) people having higher self esteem are likely to experience higher level of satisfaction both in work and non work place. Further, Cutrona (1982) reported the people with low self esteem to experience virtually every negative emotion more commonly than those with higher self esteem.

On the basis of their study on the role interactions of married working women, Hemlata and Suryanarayan (1983) reported that 89.3% women liked their jobs and thought that education and employment enhanced their status. Because of this positive attitude, they had been able to combine the role of worker with that of a housewife successfully. Epstein (1983); Schooler *et al.* (1984) further added that the multiple role life style of working women allowed opportunities for personal growth and enhancement, including the financial benefits. Coleman and Antonucci (1983) also showed that women employed outside the home have higher self esteem than those who were not employed. Moreover, Pietromonaco *et al.* (1984) found higher levels of self esteem among women who occupied three roles of wife, mother and paid worker compared with women who occupied fewer roles. They did not observe any increase in reported stress associated with a greater number of roles. The more roles women occupied, the more sources of pleasure she reported in her life.

Gove and Zeiss (1987) related paid employment to the increased self esteem, efficacy perception and status in working mothers. The work place appears to offer benefits such as challenge, control, structure, positive feedback and self esteem to provide a valued set of social ties (Baruch *et al.* 1987).

Strykowska (1991) found the family and occupation to be such a fundamental component of women's image in their self esteem that they stopped thinking about family as an obstacle in their occupational activity. Further, Nathawat and Mathur (1993) found that working women scored higher on the self esteem measure than the nonworking women.

According to Baumeister (1993); Greenberg *et al.* (1992) high self esteem appears to buffer people against feelings of anxiety, enhancing coping and promoting, physical health. Similar findings have been earlier reported by Tedeschi and Norman (1985) who found that people seek self esteem because it is associated with the feelings of control over one's environment. Higher self esteem serves as a buffer against the essential anxiety people experience when the contemplate their own fragility and mortality.

Napholz (1995) identified the relationship of sex-role orientation to the indices of psychological well being among working women. Analyses revealed that sex typed group had significantly lower self esteem scores than cross types and androgynous groups. The undifferentiated group had significantly lower self esteem scores when compared with androgynous group.

However, there has been an additional important modifications of the Role Accumulation Hypothesis in the form of Role Substitution Hypothesis according to which psychological effects of a role may vary depending on the other roles a woman holds. It suggests that when two roles provide similar resources, then these roles may substitute for each other. Consequently, woman who occupies either role may benefit, but there may be additional benefit from occupying both roles. For example employment and marriage may substitute for each other as sources of income and social support (Ali and Avison, 1997). Thus, employment may have less beneficial effect on health for married women than for unmarried woman since a married woman has a husband as an alternative source of financial resources and social support.

Women, Multiple Roles, Adjustment and Quality of Life

Each social role occupied appears to have its own demands and requires adjustment on the part of women to successfully deal with them. The adjustment may be related to occupation, health, marriage, etc.

Burke and Weir (1976) found that working women scored lower on marital adjustment in lower class and at lower educational levels but that the effect of working was greatly reduced or disappeared among middle class women (Bahr and Day, 1976). However, Lewis and Spanier (1979) concluded that marital quality may be related more to the congruence between the role expectation of one spouse and the role performance of the other spouse than to any specific pattern of roles.

Yogev (1981) has shown that the tensions between work and family can lead to poor marital adjustment and inadequate role performance. Moreover, Houseknecht and Macke (1981) reported that is not the employment status per se that is important in determining marital adjustment but rather, the extent to which family accommodate the wife's employment. Marriage provides a stable, coherent and regulated environment and for the most part, married people live a healthier lifestyle than the single (Hughes and Gove, 1981). However, Smith (1985) reported no net effect of a wife's employment, occupational commitment or higher occupational prestige on marital satisfaction.

Williams *et al.* (1991) obtained immediate negative effect of multiple role juggling on task enjoyment and mood of working mothers. Their results reflected the complex nature of psychological adjustment to multiple role occupancy. However, Nathawat and Mathur (1993) indicated significantly better adjustment for the women working outside the home than for housewives.

Etzion *et al.* (1994) studied the patterns of adjustment to career/family conflict of technically trained women. The results suggested that women face a practical dilemma in combining career and family as well as family dilemma related to their identity as women.

Husain and Sharma (1994) examined the relationship between marital adjustment and trust, marital adjustment and social intimacy and trust and social intimacy among 100 Hindu and 100 Muslim women, half of each sample working outside home. Marital adjustment scores were found to be significantly correlated with trust scores among Hindu working and non-working women. Fairly high correlation were found between marital adjustment and social intimacy scores among Hindu working and non-working women. Pandey (1996) examined the effect of profession on the social and marital adjustments of the working women as compared to non-working women. Results showed significantly higher scores of non-working women on the marital adjustment than the working Ss. The social and marital lives were found to be adversely affected by the profession of women.

Singh and Bawa (1996) studied the adjustment problems

of working women. Their findings revealed teachers to be better adjusted from occupational point of view than clerks and housewives. Nurses were found to be better adjusted on home, emotional and occupational domains whereas teachers were better from the point of view of health and social adjustment.

Steyn (1997) concluded that spousal support affected both family and work adjustment of employment wives positively.

All the adjustments made by the individuals to so many stresses is guided by one basic motive to struggle for survival and for the betterment of life or to live life at its best. This may be referred to as good quality of life. The concept 'Quality of Life' (QOL) is relatively new. Although its parameters are unspecified, still some researches have tried to approach this very concept from different perspectives like life satisfaction, well being, mental health, etc.

Rose (1955) found the employed married women to have greater life satisfaction and greater self acceptance. On the contrary, Coser and Rokoff (1971) reported that both work and family provide separate source of stress which could negatively affect the well being. Furthermore, they can generate role conflict through their interaction, which could also increase psychological distress. Calhaun (1974) further pointed that family and job conditions can shape certain self perceptions and in this way affect psychological well being. Specifically, particular job and family situations can affect individual's sense of personal control which, when compromised, is associated with lower well being.

Gove and Tudor (1973) have shown that marriage can be dysfunctional to women's health. On the other hand Mostow and Newberry (1975) reported the involvement in multiple identities to have certain benefits. The association between family role stress and negative health outcomes were typically found to be less strong in employed women compared to the housewives. These results were further confirmed by Brown in 1975.

Goodman (1975) examined the differential effect of various

types of jobs on the health of employed women and found lower mortality for physicians and for high level managers and professionals in federal work force, relative to the general population.

Rodloff (1975) controlling for happiness with job and marriage found the housewives to be significantly more depressed than the working wives. These findings were supported by Pearlin *et al.* (1981) who reported more likelihood of experiencing "role disenchantment" and depression in women occupying the role of homemaker as compared with the employed. Similarly, Aneshensel (1986) suggested employed women to be less depressed than the non-employed, but this difference was not observed in other studies (Baruch and Barnett, 1986; Clearly and Mechanic, 1983). Merikangas (1985) however reported employment as a risk factor for depression in women. Gove *et al.* (1983) further found unmarried to have higher levels of depression, anxiety and other forms of psychological distress than the married. These findings were supported by Gersten *et al.* (1985) who explained that the emotional support provided by marriage decreased depression, anxiety and sickness. Menaghan (1989) however, reported sex differences in experiencing depression and found employed married mothers to be more anxious and distressed than similar fathers.

The Quality of Life for the working population has been conceptualized as derived from the satisfactions experienced through having a good job and a good life (Payton and Brayfield, 1976). Ferree (1976) found employed wives to be more satisfied than the housewives. However, Gove and Geerken (1977) reported that the employed women's psychiatric symptoms in increased with the number of children in the household.

Pearlin and Johnson (1977) strongly suggested the marriage to play an important role in producing or maintaining psychological well being under the conditions of stress. Kasl (1978) however linked both higher marital as well as job satisfaction with better mental health. The contribution of job and the leisure satisfaction to the quality of life has been examined by London *et al.* (1977). According to Kakar (1978) the women's inner experiences are inextricably embedded in the socio-economic and cultural matrix, so it is likely that the role of wage earner will bring a change in their quality of life.

Hauenstein *et al.* (1977) linked the employment and blood pressure levels and found no difference in the blood pressure levels of the working women and housewives but, the self reports of tension in the role of homemaker were linked with elevated blood pressure in housewives and not in employed women. Waldron (1978) associated high occupational status with Type A behaviour. Further links between employment, blood pressure and Type A behaviour have also been reorted by Haynes and Feinlib (1980). They found the working women with children to be more likely to develop CHD than those without children. Marcus and Seeman (1981) reported higher rates of acute illness among unemployed compared to the employed. Similarly, Rice and Cugliani (1979) reported employed people to have lower rates of acute illness, chronic conditions, constricted activities and physicians visit than non-employed people. Their results were supported by Woods and Hulka (1979) and later by Marcus *et al.* (1983) who also found employed women to be physically healthier than non-employed women. Single women were further reported to have better health than married (Jennings *et al.* 1984). In contrast Verbrugge and Madans (1985) found the healthiest women to have multiple roles—a job, a husband and often children. Earlier, Verbrugge (1983) also reported a positive relationship of multiple roles and health. Brenner and Levi (1987) further observed that among women, the employed reported best physical health, housewives reported lower health and worst health was reported by unemployed. Insignificant effects of number of children and number of hours spent in child care on self reported health of women have been reported by Bir and Fremont (1989). Waldron and Jacobs (1989) also found that for white middle aged women, the effects of labour force participation on self reported general health did not differ for those who had children and those who did not. These findings got further support from Hughes (1998) who found neither having children nor the longer hours of employment to have any harmful effect on health of women. Asuncion *et al.* (1993) concluded that the employed mothers reported better mental health adjustment than their counterparts.

Woods (1978) found that in the absence of support from significant others, women's involvement in multiple roles had a deleterious effect on their mental health. Uneven sharing of the burdens (in terms of family and social obligations) by women, with the additional pressures experienced therefrom have been further shown to affect their work and life satisfaction (Jones and Butler, 1980). These findings contradicted the earlier results of Spreitzer *et al.* (1979) who reported the occupancy of multiple roles to increase social involvement and personal achievement with which individuals may feel more satisfied about their lives. La Rocco *et al.* (1980) also emphasized work and family to provide separate source of social support as well as self fulfillment and that each could contribute independently to psychological well being. Higher levels of life satisfaction (Stewart and Salt, 1981) and physically well being (Verbrugge, 1982) among the women occupying three roles of wife, mother and paid worker have been shown.

Married women with children in home have been found to have higher psychiatric symptom levels and worse health than those without children (Kessler and McCrae, 1982; Gove, 1984). Mandler (1984) further pointed that when roles are juggled, goal oriented behaviour in our domain (*e.g.* work) is interrupted by the demands from other domain (*e.g.* family). Interruption of behaviour is associated with anxiety and negative affect.

Brauch *et al.* (1985) found consistent association between the occupancy of role of wife and high marital quality with higher well being. Whereas, the mothers were found to report more symptoms of distress than women who were not mothers. It is because the responsibilities of care giving may cripple women's climb up the career ladder, while the burden of care can lead to emotional collapse, stained personal relationships and decline in physical health (Abbot and Brody, 1985). Sekran

(1983) reported job and life satisfaction as an important dimensions of quality of life. Women who desire a career for themselves are looking for the satisfactions at the work place which would be an important component of the quality of life enjoyed by them. A moderate relationship between job satisfaction and life satisfaction has also been indicated by Brief and Hollenbeck (1985) who found this relationship to be greatest for the subjects with occupation characterized as complex and high in status.

The well being in women and men has been found to increase with the number of roles undertaken (Pietromonaco *et al.,* 1986). The cross sectional research by Aneshensel and Pearlin (1987) on role occupancy indicated that employed women reported better mental health than women who were not employed. However, women's primary responsibility for children has been suggested as a factor that may account for poorer mental health of mothers compared to fathers (Rosenfield, 1989). Goldstein (1990) also found that having children did not generally improve the psychological well being of parents. However, both positive and negative effects of occupying multiple roles on mother's psychological well being have been reported (Umberson and Gove, 1989; Lambert, 1990). Umberson and Gove (1989) suggested that the negative yet modest impact of parenting on well-being may represent the balance of costs and benefits of parenting according to family life stage and context. Utilizing a national probability sample of over 2,000 respondents, they obtained data on current living arrangements of parents and children and compared several groups of parents at various life stages including variety of indicators of psychological well-being. Interestingly, Umberson and Gove (1989) found that the costs of parenting are highest when children and parents live in the same household, and children are under the age of 18. Rewards from parenting, however, outweigh costs later in the family life course, particularly when adult children live in separate residences and maintain relationships with their parents. Umberson and Gove concluded that parenting in different contexts affects well-being in different ways. With regard to gender, several interactions between gender and parental status were reported; some indicated that women were more affected by parenting than men, but others indicated the opposite.

Ross and Mirowsky (1988) contended that the effect of a wife's employment status on psychological well being depended on the presence of children, the type of Child Care (CC) available, the difficulty of arranging CC, and husband's participation in CC. Employment was found to be associated with improved mental health only among those women whose husbands shared family work. Brief and Hollenback (1985) reported that for employed wives, depression was not affected by children *per se* but by the ease or difficulty in arranging Child Care (CC) and by husband's participation in CC. For non-employed, children increased the depression levels. However, Warr and Parry (1982) did not find any negative effect of working on the well being of married women. These findings were further supported by Thoits (1983) who reported that regardless of gender, occupancy of upto seven roles was positively associated with mental health. The social cognitive theory by Bandura (1986), however, states that the well being is determined by people's belief in their efficacy or capability to mobilize the motivation, cognitive resources and courses of action needed to exercise control over given events. Further Hirsch and Rapkin (1986) reported that the perceived quality of role and responses of social network members may affect the well being of those who occupy multiple roles. Sinha (1986) assessed and compared Quality of Life (QOL) among different professionals like railway officers, bank managers and University teachers. Results revealed bank officers as having better QOL than university teachers and railway officers.

Meleis *et al.* (1989) examined the relationship of personal characteristics, role identity, sex role orientation, and role integration on perceived health and psychological status in women. Results revealed that number of roles did not predict perceived health or psychological status. Greater involvement with enacted roles was positively associated with perceived health. Role integration was found to make the most difference in perceived health and psychological status. Menaghan (1989) also asserted that specific role combination are more important than the simple number of roles in influencing psychological symptoms, and that the magnitude of psychological impact of role combinations very with normative appropriateness of roles based on gender and age.

Kahn *et al.* (1989) examined marital and parental status in relation to perceptions of the quality of work and family roles (psychological well being, job satisfaction, work involvement, non-occupational environment and role demands) in female clerks. Results showed that income differentiated married and unmarried women and the presence of school age children was related to greater role demands. Gray *et al.* (1990) further examined two aspects of well being (perceived stress and coping, and life satisfaction) of married mothers of infants working full time to determine the relationship of husband's supportiveness to their well being. Husband's psychological support for Ss dual roles and his participation in family work were most strongly associated with the ability to cope with stress and life satisfaction.

Helson *et al.* (1990) showed that women's role involvement affected their psychological well being and that role quality was a more important factor than role quantity in predicting women's well being. The quality of employed women's experience in the home making role and its relationship to their psychological well being and distress was examined by Kibria *et al.* (1990). A favourable association of positive homemaking role quality with psychological well being was found. The distress was enhanced by positive paid work role quality, suggesting that the relationship of home making role quality to psychological outcomes was influenced by the effects of paid work role quality on psychological well being and distress. Barnett *et al.* (1992) also indicated that women who reported high levels of job, partner or parent quality, reported low levels psychological symptoms. However, Thoits (1992) suggested the combination of roles occupied and the gender holding the roles to have significant consequences for psychological well being.

Researches by Bandura (1991); Ozer and Bandura (1990)

indicated that perceived self efficacy mediated the relationship between the psychological variables and mental health. A sense of low coping efficacy has been found to contribute to anxiety, negative thinking and depression. Amatea and Fong (1991) also suggested that professional women with greater perceived control report fewer psychological symptoms than women with less perceived control.

Walker and Best (1991) compared the well of employed women and homemakers, both having infant children and found that employed Ss reported greater stress in their lives and less healthy lifestyles than homemakers. Employed Ss life styles showed diminished attention to their own personal health and well being. However, Lennon and Rosenfield (1992) reported that employed women with greater job control experienced significantly greater psychological well being than housewives. In contrast, women whose occupation were characterized by low control did not differ significantly from homemakers.

Higgins *et al.* (1992) found that work interfering with family was related to lower quality of family life which in turn was related to lower levels of life satisfaction among workers. But, Beehr and McGrath (1992) have contended that social support provided by members of work and / or family domains can have a positive influence on person's general well being.

Aston and Lavery (1993) further studied the effects of quality of work role, social support and cynicism on psychological and physical well being. They examined the possible benefits of the work place experience for women in term of rewards and concerns intrinsic to the job, reward and concern extrinsic to the job and social support. While the intrinsic factors were found to be generally related to psychological well being, the extrinsic factors were more closely related to physical being.

Lennon *et al.* (1994) explored the sources and consequences of employed wives perceptions of fairness in the division of housework. Findings suggested that women who had fewer alternatives to marriage and less economic resources were more likely to view a given division of housework as fair, while women with more alternatives viewed the same division as unjust. Also, women who perceived an unequal situation as fair experienced lower psychological well being. He further compared the employed wives and full time homemakers on characteristics of their daily work activities and on the consequences of work conditions for psychological well being and reported that full time housework involved more autonomy, more interruptions, greater physical effort, more routine, fewer time pressures and less responsibility for matters outside one's control than did paid work. Full time homemakers appeared to benefit from having less responsibility for things outside their control as compared to employed wives whereas, employed wives appeared to benefit from having less routinized work than homemakers. Employed wives and homemakers on an average experienced similar levels of depressive symptoms. However, Thakar and Misra (1995) found that dual career women reported significantly greater incidence of daily hassles but displayed a greater degree of life satisfaction than did the housewives.

Wharton (1995) investigated the relations between women's job and family emotion work and the effects of both on women's job related well being. Results showed that performance of family emotion work had negative consequences for women's job related well being. While Ss involvement in emotion work resulted in lower job related well being, these negative consequences stemmed from family emotion work they performed rather then from their performance of emotional labour on the job. Greater child care responsibility was associated with lower well being and greater psychological distress. Perceived self efficacy to cope with the demands of occupational and familial roles appeared to mediate this relationship (Ozer, 1995).

Burke and Mc Keen (1995) examined a research model developed to understand emotional well being among managerial and professional women most of whom were in early career, married but still without children. Work experiences and work outcomes were found to be fairly consistently and significantly related to self reported emotional well being. Noor (1995) tested three-way interaction between job role quality, locus of control and support in relation to two measures of women's psychological well being : happiness and symptoms of distress.

Pattison and Moyse (1995) reported suitability for occupation as a better indicator of psychological strain among mothers than their employed status alone. Noor (1997) pointed that the wives estimates of their husbands time spent doing housework was a better predict of their well being than their estimates of their own time spent. Moreover, support was found to act as a partial mediator in this relationship.

Aminah (1996) reported work family conflict and less life satisfaction among working women. Non-working experienced greater life satisfaction and happiness than working women (Saxena, 1996). On the contrary Rani and Yadav (2000) reported lesser anxiety among working women than non-working women inspite of thie dual responsibilities and stressors. Singh (1997) revealed age as well as working conditions of women having significant influence on anxiety. Haworth *et at.* (1997) emphasized valued position in both work and leisure to have important associations with positive psychological states. Internal locus of control was found to be associated with greater enjoyment, life satisfaction and effective well being.

Devi and Kumari (1997) examined the relationship between socio-economic status of nurses and perception of their life satisfaction Results suggested that socio-economic status did not significantly predict life satisfaction.

Working women have been found to have sound mental health than the housewives (Vijaylaxmi and Kulkarni, 2000). Although women who work outside the home, are required to make many social readjustments a good job can contribute to overall quality of life through increased income and more satisfying experiences than available to a traditional housewife (Kumari and Singh, 2000).

Studies reviewed in this context present a rather contradictory picture. While some studies suggested non-working women to experience greater anxiety and stress than the working women, there are others which reported work family conflict and less life satisfaction among working women. Similarly, with regard to the social (familial) role there have been some studies which have shown the married women reporting better health (Verbrugge, 1987) supporting role accumulation hypothesis whereas others have found single women to fair better then the married women (Jennings *et al.,* 1984); still others have reported little or no effect of marital status (Baruch and Barnett, 1986). Rankin (1993) however reported the employed mothers to be more stressed and hence supporting role strain hypothesis. Study by Frone (1992), however, other hand provided support to role complementation hypothesis by reporting the combinations of career and family roles to be associated with role conflict and stress.

Not only being employed but also the professions in which employed may determines the psychological state of women. Again the findings from different studies in this regard are incongruent. Pandey (1996) reported adverse effects of being in different professions on social and marital lives of women whereas Haworth (1997) emphasized valued position in both work and leisure to have important associations with positive psychological states. The picture emerging out of these findings is rather conflicting. Moreover, while the main thrust appears to be on studying marital adjustment, the adjustment of women in various other fronts like home, social, emotional etc. have been largely ignored. Regarding the quality of life, studies using and exclusive parameter for measuring quality of life are scanty. Quality of life of working and non- working women in different domains has also not been attended to in past researches. Since the problems and difficulties of women are multidimensional, they need further probing. Thus, with the purpose of exploring the psychological consequences of multiplicity of social roles in working women the present study was carried out with three principle objectives :

1. To compare working and non-working women on self esteem adjustment and quality of life.
2. To study the impact of multiplicity of social roles and professions on role conflict, self esteem, adjustment and quality of life of working women.
3. To generate an equation in predicting quality of life of working women in different domains.

It was hypothesized that :

1. Working and non-working women would differ significantly on their self esteem, level of adjustment and quality of life.
2. There would be an increase in the role conflict with the increasing level of social roles.
3. More the number of social (familial) roles occupied by working women higher would be their self esteem.
4. Number of social roles would significantly effect the level of adjustment in different domains (home, health, social, emotional, occupational).
5. Multiple social roles of working women would have varied effects on different domains of QOL (physical, psychological, social and environmental).
6. Level of adjustment, quality of life (QOL), role conflict and self esteem of women would differ in relation to there professions.
7. There would be an interactive effect of professions and social (familial) roles on the different dependent variables.

The following chapter will address the design and methodology of the present study including the selection of participants, research procedures and description of instruments.

3 DESIGN AND METHODOLOGY

For testing the hypotheses formulated in chapter II, the study was conducted in two phases and it was designed in the following manner :

DESIGN

Phase-I

Two group design was employed for the global assessment of differences between working and non-working women on their self esteem, adjustment and quality of life (QOL).

Group 1 (Working Women)	Group 2 (Non-working Women)	
n=50	n=50	N=100

Phase-II

A 3×3 factorial design was used to have a closer look into the net effect of multiplicity of social (familial) roles (unmarried, married, married with children) professions (doctors, lecturers, nurses) and their interactive effect on role conflict, self esteem, adjustment and quality of life.

Regarding the number of social roles, subjects were assigned a role level depending on their number of roles in family. Each role level consisted of only one specific role or set of roles. The three role levels were-working unmarried (1), working married (2), working, married and mother (3). Professions were varied on perceived social recognition.

Sample

Although, the women of today can be seen working in almost all the professions. Since it is beyond the scope of a single

		Levels of Social (Familial) Roles			
		Level-1 (Unmarried)	Level-2 (Married)	Level-3 (Married with children)	
Professions as varied on perceived social recognition	High (Doctors)	n=30	n=30	n=30	90
	Moderate (Lecturers)	n=30	n=30	n=30	90
	Low (Nurses)	n=30	n=30	n=30	90
		90	90	90	N=270

research to study all these professionals, therefore, it was essential to limit the professions from which the sample would be drawn. It was rather difficult to decide which professions to opt for and which one to leave. For this purpose a checklist was hence prepared comprising of different professions in which women are more likely to be involved like banking, medical, teaching, administrative/executives, secretaries, nursing, etc. A survey was then conducted among the general population (N=250) to rate these professions on 3 point scale (low, moderate and high) in terms of their perceived social recognition.

Out of the population surveyed 75% rated doctors in high category lecturers/teachers were rated in moderate category by 72% people and 67% rated nurses in low category of percieved social recognition. Because of reasonably high percentage of people agreeing on the above mentioned categories, these three distinct groups of professionals were chosen for the inclusion in the sample. To make it more comprehensive, the professionals serving in government institutes were included. The sample of doctors, nurses and lecturers was drawn from PGIMS, Rohtak, civil hospitals and different government colleges respectively of Rohtak and nearby districts in Haryana. After collecting information regarding their age, marital status and income, a list was prepared of only those professionals who were within the age group of 25-45 years. These professional women were further fabricated into three categories of social (familial) roles *i.e.,* unmarried, married and married with children. 30 subjects from each of these categories were then selected randomly. However, extra 10 subjects were selected in order to avoid the uncertainty regarding their availability.

Besides this, a sample of 50 educated housewives (atleast graduates) between the age group of 25-45 years were selected as the comparison group. In all, the total sample comprised of 320 Ss (270 working and 50 non-working women).

Measures

The following materials/tools were used in the present study :

1. Demographic Questionnaire.
2. Role Conflict Scale (Dr. A. Pandey).
3. Self Esteem Inventory—Adult Form (S. Coppersmith, 1981).
4. The Adjustment Inventory—Adult Form (H.M. Bell, 1961).
5. WHO QOL-BREF (Quality of Life Scale, field version, 1996 WHO).

1. Demographic Questionnaire

The demographic questionnaire asked participants to indicate their age, marital status, monthly income, family size, family structure (nuclear/joint). Number and age of children were also assessed. With regard to paid employment, the questionnaire asked participants to indicate number of hours worked per day, length of service in present organization, etc.

2. Role Conflict Scale (Dr. A. Pandey)

This is a self administering inventory. Though it may be used individually, it may also be given to groups of any reasonable size. There is no time limit for the test. However, most of the groups finish it in about thirty minutes,. The role conflict scale comprises of thirty statements. There are five category response choices for each statement, *i.e.* Strongly Agree, Agree,

Undecided, Disagree and Strongly disagree. The statements are written in both positive and negative directions.

The subject's total score is considered as the role conflict score. A high score on the scale indicates a high level of role conflict while a low score shows a low level of role conflict. A low level of role conflict would be better for good performance and satisfaction.

The primary and the proper usefulness of the scale lies with the work on large groups, whether for research, survey purposes, or for comparison of population working in organizations etc. As role conflict is a common problem found in different employees, this scale can be successfully used for screening out employees who suffer from high degree of role conflict. Low score, *i.e.* below 25th percentile could be regarded as indicative of poor role conflict. Very high scores on it, *i.e.* above the 75th percentile may be considered as symptomatic of such high state of role conflict which is likely to have a disruptive and interfering influence on the performance. The middle group of scores would represent essentially 'normal' individuals, with moderately good drive level to stimulate performance without itself proving as interference.

The scale constitutes a useful research tool. It is eminently suitable for individual testing as well as for group administration.

The scale has been developed and standardized on an Indian sample. Test-retest and split half reliabilities have been computed for this scale, both of which were found to be very high *i.e.,* .87 and .79 respectively. Criterion related validity has also been determined. Role conflict scale (Risso House and Lirtzman 1970) was used as a criterion scale. The correlation co-efficient between criterion scale and the present scale was found to be .81.

3. Self Esteem Inventory-Adult Form (S. Coopersmith, 1981)

The Self Esteem Inventory (SEI) is designed to measure evaluative attitudes towards the self. All SEI items are short statements. The adult form is used with the persons aged sixteen and above. It consists of twenty five items adapted from the school short form. The correlation of total scores on the school short form and the adult form exceeds .80. The adult form is usually self administered and the administration time rarely exceeds ten minutes. Scoring is done by using the scoring key. In case of non-availability of scoring key, the general rules listed below are followed :

- Negative items are scored "correct" if they have been answered "Unlike me".
- Positive items are scored "correct" if they have been answered "like me".

SEI may be used for Individual Assessment, Instructional Planning, Programme Evaluation or for clinical and research studies. By administering the SEI to an individual or to a group, a general assessment of high, medium or low self esteem can be obtained. Cutoff points can be established and persons with scores above or below those points can be identified for further evaluation. A person's SEI results may also be examined on an item-by-item basis to locate particular areas in need of development. It can be used on a pre/post basis to judge the effectiveness of self esteem programmes.

4. The Adjustment Inventory—Adult Form (H.M. Bell, 1961)

This inventory comprises of 160 statements. There is no time limit. Ordinarily not more than twenty five minutes are required for all individual to complete the inventory.

The inventory has been successfully used as an aid in counselling adults whose personal problems pertain to any of the categories included in the test. It is suitable for the use with both sexes. The high reliabilities of the separate measures make possible comparison of one individual with another. The measurement of five types of adjustment by the one blank permits location of specific adjustment difficulties. The used of the small letters a, b, c, d and e corresponding to the five measures of adjustment, as well as numbers, enables the counselor to develop readily the particular questions relating to each measure. The total score is used to indicate the general adjustment status. The interpretation of individual scores is made more meaningful by the use of certain descriptive designations.

The inventory has been validated in two ways : First, the items for each of the sections in the inventory were selected in terms of degree to which they differentiated between the upper and lower fifteen percent of the individuals in a distribution of adult scores. Only those items which clearly differentiated between these extreme groups are included in the present form of the inventory. Second, the inventory has been validated through the selection of "very well" and "very poorly" adjusted groups of individuals by specialists in adult counselling and determination of the degree to which the inventory differentiates among them.

The co-efficients of reliability for each of the five sections of the inventory and for its total score have been determined by correlating the odd-even items and applying the Spearman-Brown prophecy formula. Co-efficients of reliability are .91 for home adjustment .81, .88, .91 and .85 for health adjustment, social adjustment, emotional adjustment and occupational adjustment, respectively. For the total score co-efficients of reliability is. 94.

Norms have been given for adults of both sexes. The individuals ranged in age from twenty to fifty years with majority falling between twenty five and forty. In determining the norms for occupational adjustment, housewives and unemployed were eliminated.

5. World Health Organization Quality of Life (WHO QOL)-BREF

The questionnaire has been developed by world health organization group in 1996 in order to provide a short form quality of life assessment that looks at Domain level profiles. It is an abbreviated 26 item assessment and contains 2 items from the overall QOL and general health and one item from each of the 24 facets included in WHO QOL-100 for providing broad and comprehensive assessment. Each item is rated on a five point scale. The questionnaire assesses quality of life in 4 domains, namely, physical health, psychological, social relationships, environment.

The WHO QOL-BREF is self administered questionnaire. The questionnaire (field trial version) produces a quality of life profile. It is possible to derive four domain scores which denote an individual's perception of quality of life in each particular domain. There are also two items which are examined separately : question 1 asks about an individual's overall perception of quality of life and question 2 asks about individual's overall perception of their health.

WHO QOL-BREF domains

Domains	*Facets incorporated within domains*
1. Physical Health	— Activities of daily living
	— Dependence on medicinal substances and medical aid
	— Energy and fatigue
	— Mobility
	— Pain and discomfort
	— Sleep and rest
	— Work capacity
2. Psychological	— Bodily image and appearance
	— Negative feelings
	— Positive feelings
	— Self esteem
	— Spirituality / religion / personal beliefs
	— Thinking, learning, memory and concentration
3. Social Relationships	— Personal relationships
	— Social support
	— Sexual activity
4. Environment	— Financial resources
	— Freedom, physical safety and security
	— Health and social care : accessibility and quality
	— Home environment
	— Opportunities for acquiring new information and skills
	— Participation in and opportunities for recreation / leisure activities
	— Physical environment (pollution / noise) traffic / climate)
	— Transport

Where more than 20% data are missing from an assessment, the assessment is discarded. Where upto two items are missing from the domain, the mean of other items in the domain is substituted. Where more than two items are missing from the domain, the domain score is not calculated (with the exception of domain 3, where data is calculated only if ≤1 item is missing).

The scale has been shown to have good discriminant validity, sound content validity and good test-retest reliability. Despite the heterogeneity of facets included within domains, all domains display excellent internal consistency. Cronbach alpha values for each of the four domain scores ranged from .66 (for domain 3) to .84 (for domain 1). The WHO QOL-BREF has many uses, including use in medical practice, policy making, research, audit and in assessing the effectiveness and relative merits of different treatments. It can also be used to assess variation in quality of life across different cultures, to compare subgroups within the same culture and to measure change across time in response to change in life circumstances.

Procedure

The selected sample of the professionals were contacted personally at their place of work. The purpose of the study was explained to them and their consent was sought for the participation in the research. After assuring them regarding the anonymity of the results, different questionnaires (Self Esteem Inventory, Role Conflict Scale, Bell's Adjustment Inventory, WHO QOL-BREF) were distributed to them separately. Besides this, socio-demographic data was also obtained for each subject. Though, all the questionnaires were self administered but for the sake of clarity with regard to the administration, the general instructions as mentioned in Annexure A were read out to them. The subjects were requested to fill the questionnaire on the same day but if due to some earlier commitment, they showed their inability for doing so, and average time of one week was allotted to them for the same. While collecting the questionnaires back on the due dates the subjects were provided opportunity to express their views regarding any aspect of the study. The questionnaires were then scored according to the scoring keys or the procedure given in the manual.

In case of the Role Conflict Scale the statements were written in both positive and negative directions. Therefore, a subject's strongly agreeing responses to the statements describing very high level of role conflict were scored 5 and strongly disagreeing to the same as 1. Conversely, strongly disagreeing responses to some statements (*i.e.* statement no : 1, 5, 7, 8, 14, 18, 22 and 24) reflecting very high level of role conflict were assigned on weight of 5 whereas strongly agreeing to the same as 1. In this way subjects responses were scored 5, 4, 3, 2 and 1 for strongly agree, agree, undecided, disagree and strongly disagree respectively for all items except for no. 1, 5, 7, 8, 14, 18, 22 and 24.

For the Self Esteem Inventory scoring was done by using the scoring key. The number of the items answered correctly were summed in order to arrive at the total raw score. It was then multiplied by four that resulted in a maximum possible Total Self Score of 100. The high scores corresponded to high self esteem.

The Bell's Adjustment Inventory (Adult Form) was also scored with the help of scoring key. The Adult Form of the Adjustment Inventory provided five separate measures of personal and social adjustment :

Home Adjustment : Individuals scoring high tended to be unsatisfactorily adjusted to their home surroundings. Low scores indicated satisfactory home adjustment.

Health Adjustment : High scores indicated unsatisfactory health adjustment; low scores, satisfactory adjustment.

Social Adjustment : Individuals scoring high tended to be submissive and retiring in their social contacts. Individuals with low scores were aggressive in social contacts.

Emotional Adjustment : Individuals with high scores tended to be unstable emotionally. Persons with low scores tended to be emotionally stable.

Occupational Adjustment : Individuals with high scores tended to be dissatisfied with the present occupation. Those who made low scores tended to be well pleased with their present jobs.

To obtain the score on Home Adjustment, the scoring stencil entitled "Home" was taken and the column for page 2 was laid on page 2 of the Inventory so that the "2" at the top and at the bottom of the stencil were superimposed upon the corresponding figures of the test. Then, the number of instances where the vertical marks on the scoring stencil fell immediately over a circle on the test were counted and this total was written at the bottom of page two. Similarly, the column on the stencil for page three was applied to the third page of the inventory and the column for page four to fourth page. The total of the three pages thus derived were written opposite "a" in the column entitled "score" on the first page of the blank. The question marks were not scored.

For the scoring of WHO QOL–BREF, two items *i.e.,* question 1 relate to an individual's overall perception of quality of life and question 2 which asked about individual's overall perception of their health, were examined separately. Moreover, four domain scores were calculated. Domain scores were scaled in positive direction (*i.e.,* higher scores denoted higher quality of life. The scoring was reversed in case of negatively phrased items. Mean cores of items within each domain was used to calculate the domain score. Mean scores was then multiplied by 4 in order to make domain scores comparable with the scores used in WHO QOL–100 and subsequently transformed to a 0-10 scale, using the following formula :

Transformed score= (Score – 4) x (100/16)

Research questions and hypotheses were answered with a variety of statistical tests. Results of these statistical analyses have been tabulated in next chapter.

4 INTERPRETATION OF RESULTS

The present chapter will statistically interpret the pertaining to the hypotheses set forth in the study. Subsequently the results would be related to the existing literature.

Although the focus of study was on the working women involved in different professions but in the first phase of the study a comparison was made between working and non-working women on self esteem, adjustment and quality of life to gather some basic information regarding the differences, if any, between these two groups (N=100).

The scores were obtained by these two groups on different questionnaires after which their means were calculated which have been presented in Fig. 4.1 , 4.2 and 4.3.

t-test were applied to see if the mean differences between these two groups were significant (Table 4.1). It is clear from Table 4.1 that the working women differed significantly on self esteem, all but one measure of adjustment and on domains of QOL except for the social relationship.

As clear from Table 4.1, the working and non-working women differed significantly on self esteem (t=2.63). Results suggested working women to have higher self esteem than their counterparts.

These results have been supported by Antonucci (1983) who found women employed outside the home having higher self esteem than those who are not employed. Similarly, Gove and Zeiss (1987) also related paid employment to increases self esteem in working women.

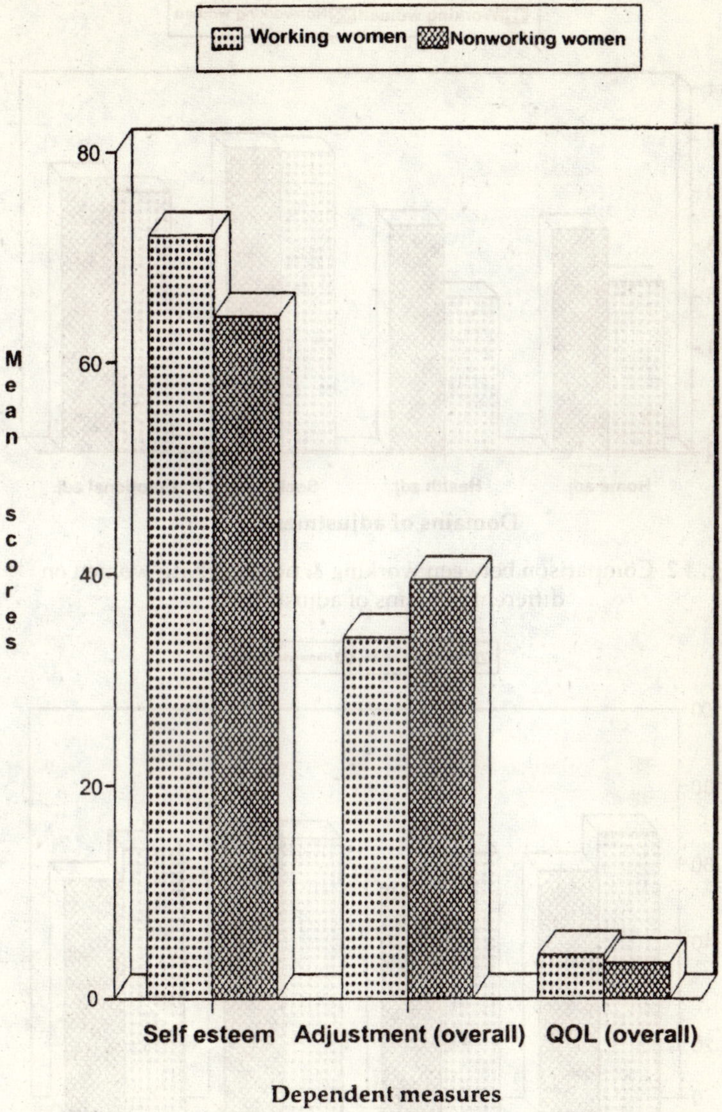

Fig. 4.1. Comparison between working & non-working women on measures of self esteem, adjustment and quality of life.

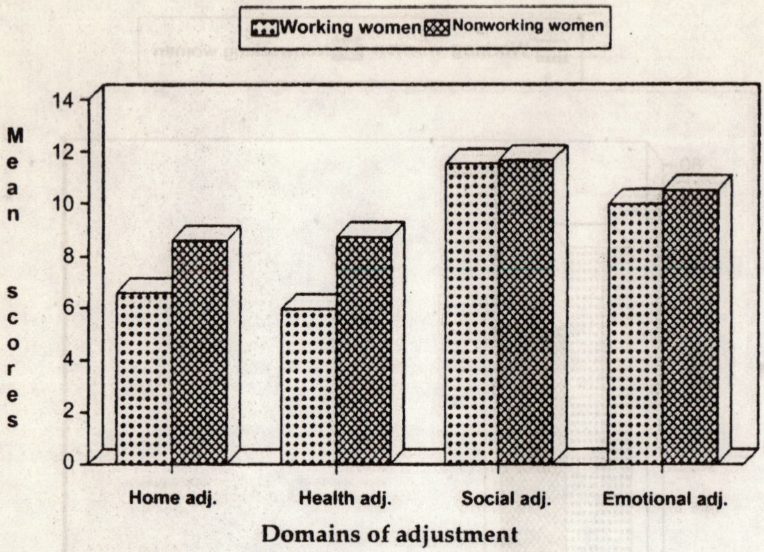

Fig. 4.2. Comparison between working & non-working women on different domains of adjustment.

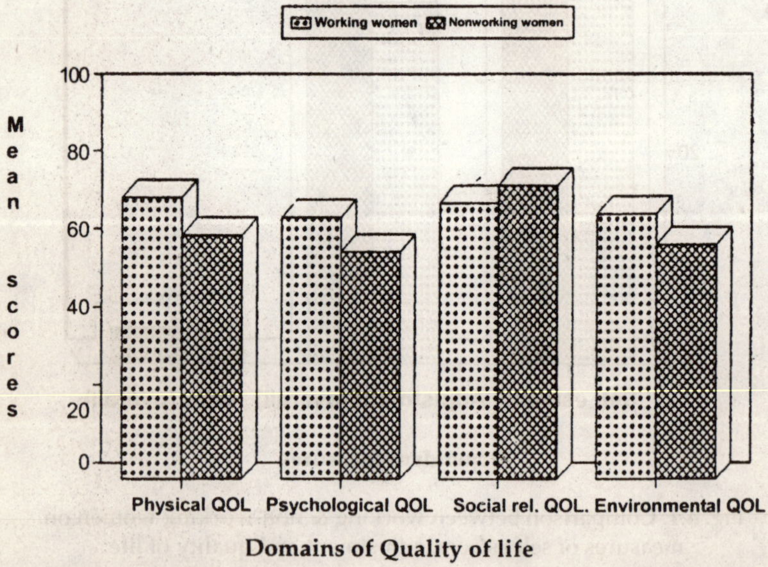

Fig. 4.3. Comparison between working & non-working women on different domains of quality of life (QOL).

Table 4.1
Comparison Between Working Women and Non-Working Women on Self Esteem, Adjustment and Quality of Life

Dependent Variables	*Working Women Mean Scores*	*Non-Working Women Mean Scores*	*t value*
Self Esteem	72	64.32	2.63**
Adjustment# (Overall)	33.98	39.42	1.995*
Home Adjustment	6.56	8.58	2.54*
Health Adjustment	5.96	8.72	3.92**
Social Adjustment	11.5	11.64	.1599
Emotional Adjustment	9.96	10.48	.5114
QOL (Overall)	4.1	3.38	4.75**
General Health	4.0	3.44	3.77**
Physical QOL	72.357	62.714	4.15**
Psychological QOL	67.25	58.5	3.42**
Social relationships	71	75.5	1.438
Environmental QOL	68.125	60.375	2.759**

* Significant at .05 level.
** Significant at .01 level.
# Inverse scoring pattern-higher the scores, unsatisfactory the adjustment

Regarding adjustment the mean scores of working and non-working were interpreted descriptively as well as the quantitatively. Although on the overall adjustment, both the working and non-working women were found to be in the average category but statistical analysis showed a significant difference between these two groups (t=1.99). Since high scores on Bell's Adjustment Inventory depicted unsatisfactory adjustment, the working women with mean adjustment score of 33.98 faired better than the non-working women (X=39.42). The comparatively poor adjustment in educated housewives may be attributed to their perception that housework is more routine and involves more contact with things and less with people than paid work does. Present results are in line with Nathawat and Mathur (1993) who indicated significantly better adjustment for women working outside the home than the housewives.

The Bell's Adjustment Inventory measured five different domains of adjustment : home, health, social, emotional and occupational. The mean scores on all these domains have been depicted in Table 4.1 and Fig. 4.2. The results indicated a significant difference between working and non-working women on home and health adjustment but no such difference was observed on social and emotional fronts (Table 4.1). At the time of administration, the housewives were instructed to leave the statements related to the occupational adjustment. Hence, no comparison could be drawn between the two groups on this domain.

Regarding quality of life, the means scores obtained by working and non-working women were 4.1 and 3.38 respectively (Fig. 4.1). The obtained t-value of 4.75 was found to be significant at 0.01 level. The mean scores of these two groups on different domains of quality of life have been tabulated in Table 4.1 and also depicted in Fig. 4.3. As evident from the Table 4.1, all the t-value excepting that of social relations QOL (t=1.438) were found to be significant.

The total picture reflected better quality of life among employed women who seemed to have more favourable perception of their lives than the non-employed women. These findings get some support from Ross and Huber (1985) who reported employed wives to have superior mental health than that of non employed wives.

Hence, the first hypothesis stating that working and non-working would differ significantly on their self esteem, level of adjustment and quality of life has been supported by present findings.

In the second phase of the study, a 3×3 factorial design was employed to study the independent as well as the interactive effect of different professions [doctors, lectures and nurses] and number of social roles [unmarried (1) married (2) and married with children (3)] on Role Conflict, Self Esteem, Adjustment and Quality of Life (QOL) of working women.

As for the Role Conflict, the raw scores were subjected to statistical analyses. Two way analysis of variance was applied and summary of the results have been presented in Table 4.2.

Table 4.2
Summary of Two Way Analysis of Variance for Role Conflict

Source of variance	*df*	*Sum of squares*	*Mean square*	*F*
Between Factor A (Professions)	2	13730.02	6865.01	47.50**
Between Factor B (Social roles)	2	3072.87	1536.43	10.63**
Interaction (A×B)	4	3614.58	903.64	6.25**
Within treatment	261	37724.4	144.54	

**Significant at 0.01 level.

As shown in the above table obtained F value for Factor A was 47.50 which far exceeded the critical value of 4.68 at 0.01 level and hence was found to be highly significant. Moreover, F, values for Factor B and AB interaction were also found to be significant at .01 level indicating that the role conflict is significantly affected by the involvement in different professions, social roles as their interaction with each other.

Since the AB interaction was found to be significant, the nature of this interaction was further studied by the presenting geometrical representations of the outcomes. For this, first the mean of the total scores were obtained (Annexure C-III) which have been graphically depicted in Fig. 4.4 and 4.5. From the mentioned Figures, it was observed that the curves marked b_1, b_2, b_3, and a_1, a_2, a_3 were not parallel, therefore the AB interaction was significant (SS_{ab}#0).

Further tests on simple effects of A and B were employed which have been shown in Tables 4.3 and 4.4 respectively.

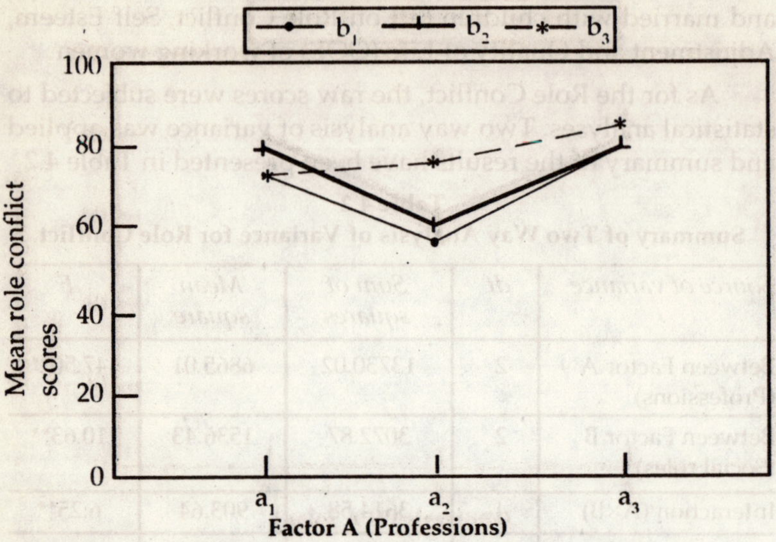

Fig. 4.4. AXB interaction profile (also profile of simple effects of factor A).

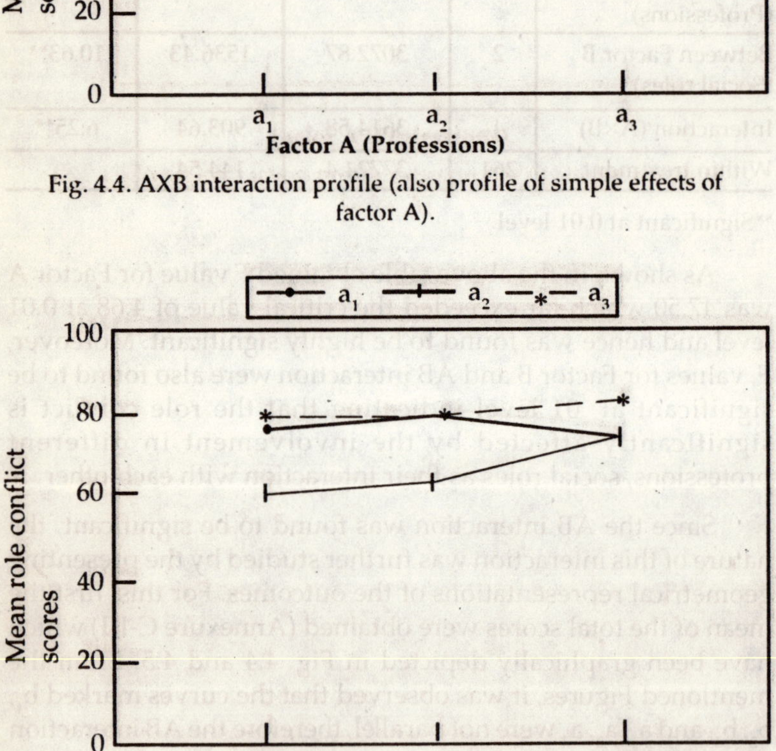

Fig. 4.5. A×B interaction profile (also profile of simple effects of factor B).

Table 4.3

Analysis of Variance for Simple Effects of A

Source of variance	*df*	*Sum of squares*	*Mean square*	*F*
A for b_1	2	7858.81	3929.41	27.18**
A for b_2	2	7158.15	3579.07	24.76**
A for b_3	2	2327.62	1163.81	8.05**
Within treatment (Error)	261	37724.4	144.54	

** Significant at 0.01 level.

Table 4.4

Analysis of Variance for Simple Effects of B

Source of variance	*df*	*Sum of squares*	*Mean square*	*F*
B for a_1	2	340.39	170.19	1.18
B for a_2	2	5417.68	2708.84	18.74**
B for a_3	2	929.39	464.70	3.21*
Within treatment (error)	261	37724.4	144.54	

* Significant at 0.05 level.

** Significant at 0.01 level.

Values of F in respect of simple effect of A for all levels of B, *i.e.* b_1, b_2, and b_3 were found to be significant (Table 4.3). It can also be observed from Fig. 4.4 that the curves representing simple effects of A for b_1, b_2, and b_3 have significant slopes. For interpreting the simple effects, it can be said that for a given level of social role (say b_1) the role conflict was maximum in case of nurses (a_3) then came the doctor (a_1) and the lectures (a_2) depicted least role conflict. At b_2 level (married social role), role conflict curves decreased upto a_2 (lectures) but then increased significantly at a_3 (nurses) showing again moderate level of role conflict in doctors, maximum in nurses and low in case of lecturers. Whereas at b_3 level (married with children) the role conflict was found to be minimum in doctors and maximum in nurses.

The F values in respect to simple effects of B were found to be significant for level a_2 and a_3 but not for a1 level (Table 4.4). Interpreting the simple effects (Fig. 4.5) it was observed that among the doctors, role conflict increased upto b_2 level (married social role) after which there was decrement in the role conflict. Whereas for lecturers and nurses the role conflict increased with the increase in the number of social roles.

The differences among the simple effects of treatment means were then tested by using Newman Keuls procedure. The test was applied on only those levels of A and B which were found to be significant (Table 4.3 and 4.4). The summary of the results have been presented in Tables 4.5 to 4.9.

Table 4.5
Schematic Summary of Results at b_1 Level (Unmarried)

a_2 *(Lecturers)*	a_1 *(Doctors)*	a_3 *(Nurses)*
57.33	75.57	78.43

Table 4.6
Schematic Summary of Results at b_2 Level (Married)

a_2 *(Lecturers)*	a_1 *(Doctors)*	a_3 *(Nurses)*
60.47	79.23	79.53

Table 4.7
Schematic Summary of Results at b_3 Level (Married with Children)

a_1 *(Doctors)*	a_2 *(Lecturers)*	a_3 *(Nurses)*
74.77	75.13	85.73

The table make it clear that in both unmarried as well as married level of social roles, the lecturers had significantly less role conflict than doctors and nurses. Nurses differed significantly from both doctors and lectures at the third level of social roles whereas, no significant difference was observed between the doctors and lecturers at this level. Nurses were found to experience maximum role conflict at all levels of social roles.

The comparison among treatment means at a_2 and a_3 levels have been presented in following tables.

Table 4.8

Schematic Summary of Results at a_2 Level (Lecturers)

b_1 (Unmarried)	*b_2 (Married)*	*b_3 (Married with children)*
57.33	60.47	75.13

Table 4.9

Schematic Summary of Results at a_3 Level (Nurses)

b_1 (Unmarried)	*b_2 (Married)*	*b_3 (Married with children)*
78.43	79.53	85.73

In both lecturers and nurses no significant difference was observed among the unmarried and married in terms of experiencing role conflict while married with children had significantly more role conflict their counterparts.

Simply stating, doctors occupying any level of the social roles *i.e.,* unmarried, married or married and mothers did not differ significantly from each other terms of experiencing role conflict. Role conflict however was maximum at the third level of social role (married with children) in case of lecturers and nurses.

Hence, the second hypothesis stating that there would be an increase in the role conflict with the increasing number of social roles is hereby partially supported by the present findings.

These results are consonant with Emmons (1990) who reported that disproportionate share of household and child care responsibilities in working mothers resulted in home and work responsibilities being placed in opposition to one another and hence leading to role conflict. A relatively old study (Hall, 1972) also supported the present findings in which married women participating in multiple roles were found to run the risk of experiencing conflict among these roles.

Further, the Self Esteem of these working women was assessed. Two way analysis of variance was first employed, the summary of which has been given in Table 4.10.

Table 4.10
Summary of Two Way Analysis of Variance for Self Esteem

Source of variance	*df*	*Sum of squares*	*Mean square*	*F*
Between Factor A (Professions)	2	11586.75	5793.38	30.07**
Between Factor B (Social roles)	2	685.06	342.53	1.78
Interaction (A×B)	4	1940.98	485.25	2.52*
Within treatment	261	50286	192.67	

* Significant at 0.05 level.
** Significant at 0.01 level.

The obtained F values for Factor A and the interaction (A×B) were significant hence implying significant effect of different professions and their interaction with level of social on the self esteem.

For the second factor *i.e.,* social (familial) roles the F value of 1.78 was not found to be significant at 0.05 and level revealing that social (familial) roles when taken alone did not have any effect on the self esteem.

The nature of this interaction has been represented in Fig. 4.6 and 4.7 which is based on the means from cell totals given in AB interaction table.

The significance of simple effects of Factor A and B were than tested and the results have been summarized in Table 4.11 and 4.12.

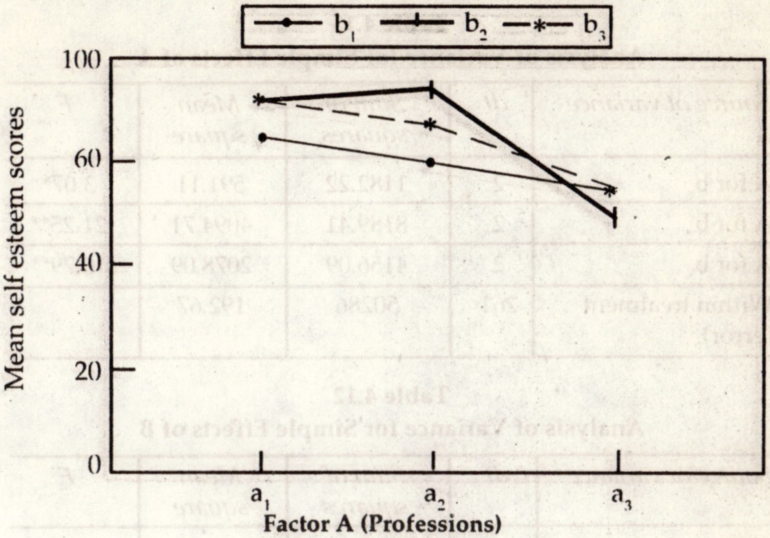

Fig. 4.6. A×B interaction profile (also profile of simple effects of factor A).

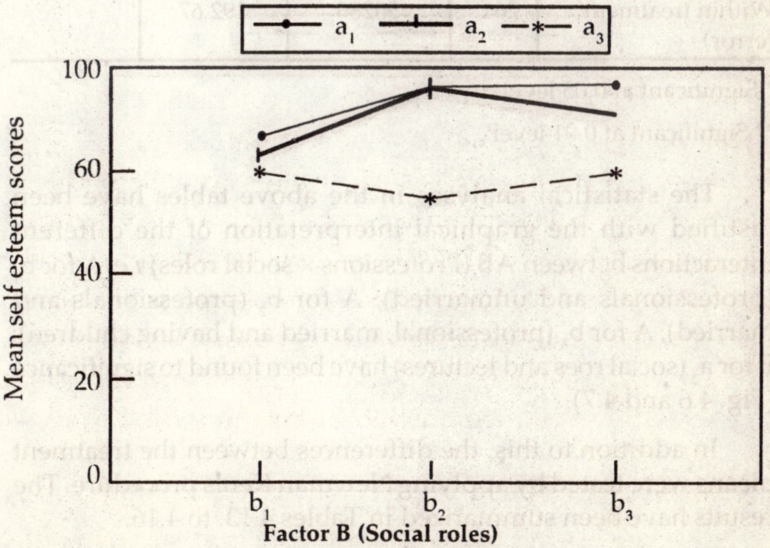

Fig. 4.7. AXB interaction profile (also profile of simple effects of factor B).

Table 4.11
Analysis of Variance for Simple Effects of A

Source of variance	*df*	*Sum of squares*	*Mean square*	*F*
A for b_1	2	1182.22	591.11	3.07*
A for b_2	2	8189.41	4094.71	21.25**
A for b_3	2	4156.09	2078.09	10.79**
Within treatment (error)	261	50286	192.67	

Table 4.12
Analysis of Variance for Simple Effects of B

Source of variance	*df*	*Sum of squares*	*Mean square*	*F*
B for a_1	2	865.69	432.84	2.25
B for a_2	2	1324.08	662.04	3.44*
B for a_3	2	436.26	218.13	1.13
Within treatment (error)	261	50286	192.67	

* Significant at 0.05 level.

** Significant at 0.01 level.

The statistical analyses in the above tables have been justified with the graphical interpretation of the different interactions between AB (Professions × social roles) *i.e.* A for b_1 (professionals and unmarried); A for b_2 (professionals and married); A for b_3 (professional, married and having children); B for a_2 (social roes and lectures) have been found to significance (Fig. 4.6 and 4.7).

In addition to this, the differences between the treatment means were tested by applying Newman Keuls procedure. The results have been summarized in Tables 4.13. to 4.16.

Table 4.13

Schematic Summary of Results at b_1 Level (Unmarried)

a_3 *(Nurses)*	a_2 *(Lectures)*	a_1 *(Doctors)*
58.93	64.93	67.6

Table 4.14

Schematic Summary of Results at b_2 Level (Married)

a_3 *(Nurses)*	a_1 *(Lectures)*	a_2 *(Doctors)*
53.87	73.93	74.27

Table 4.15

Schematic Summary of Results at b_3 Level (Married with Children)

a_3 *(Nurses)*	a_2 *(Lectures)*	a_1 *(Doctors)*
58.00	68.67	74.40

The above tables explain the difference among simple effects of A means at different levels of B. As evident, at all the levels of social roles nurses had significantly lower self esteem. Doctors showed higher self esteem at level b_1 (Unmarried) and b_3 (Married with children) whereas lectures were found to have significantly higher self esteem than nurses at the b_2 (married) level. However, no significant difference was found to exist between doctors and lectures at any level of social roles. The differences among simple effects of B at a_2 level were than studies, results of which have been summaries below.

Table 4.16

Schematic Summary of Results at a_2 Level (Lecturers)

b_1 *(Unmarried)*	b_3 *(Married with children)*	b_2 *(Married)*
64.93	68.67	74.27

Within the lectures, the married were found to be significantly higher on self esteem than those who were unmarried, whereas, no significant difference was observed between married lectures and those who were also mothers. No comparisons were made at a_1 and a_3 level due to insignificant F values for these levels (Table 4.12)

These results on the Self Esteem measure suggested that while professions had significant effect on the self esteem of working women, occupy of different social roles did not have significant effect independently but had significant effect while interacting with the different professions.

Hence, the third hypothesis stating that more the number of social (familial) roles occupied by working women, higher would be their self esteem has not been supported by the presented findings.

These findings have been partially supported by Strykowska (1991) who found both family and occupation to be a fundamental component of women's image in their self esteem. However, the present results are contradictory to Pietromonaco *et at.* (1984) who reported higher levels of self esteem among women occupying three roles of wife, mother and paid worker compared with women occupying fewer roles.

The adjustment of the working women regard to their professions and levels of social roles was then studied. The summary of two way analysis of variance has been given in Table 4.17.

The table makes it clear that F value for Factor A was significant at 0.01 level indicating that different professions significantly effected the adjustment of women. F-value for Factor B did not exceed the critical value of 3.03 at 0.05 level revealing no significant independent effect of social roles on adjustment. For the AB interaction the obtain F value was found to exceed the critical value of 3.38 at 0.01 level and thus, was significant indicating the interactive effect of different professions and levels of different social roles on the overall adjustment of working women.

Table 4.17

Summary of Two Way Analysis of Variance for Adjustment

Source of variance	*df*	*Sum of squares*	*Mean square*	*F*
Between Factor A	2	11960.27	5980.14	24.02**
Between Factor B	2	1130.36	565.18	2.27
Interaction (A×B)	4	3511.39	877.85	3.52**
Within treatment	261	64985.07	248.98	

** Significant at 0.01 level.

The AB interaction has been further depicted graphically for Fig. 4.8 and 4.9.

Since the low scores on Bell's Adjustment Inventory depicted satisfactory adjustment, therefore it can be safely said that at first and second level of social roles (Fig 4.8) the lecturers were more satisfactorily adjusted than either doctors or nurses (b_1 to b_2 curves). However, at the third level of social roles (married with children), the doctors were found to be better adjusted while nurses were found to be the most unsatisfactory adjusted groups at all three levels of social roles.

Decrement in the a_1 curve at higher levels of social roles indicating satisfactory adjustment among doctors occupying more number of social roles. However, the adjustment of nurses and lectures was unsatisfactory at higher levels of social roles (Fig. 4.9).

The analysis proceeded further by applying the tests on simple effects. The results have been summarized in Tables 4.18 and 4.19.

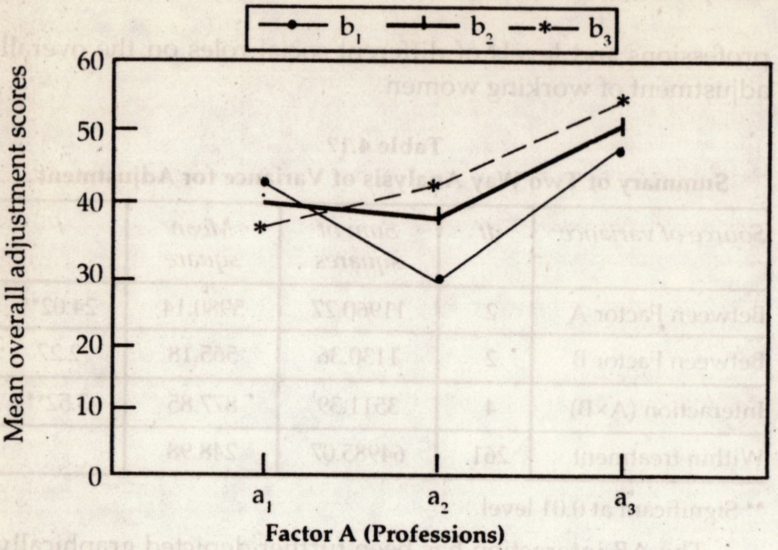

Fig. 4.8. A×B interaction profile (also profile of simple effects of factor A).

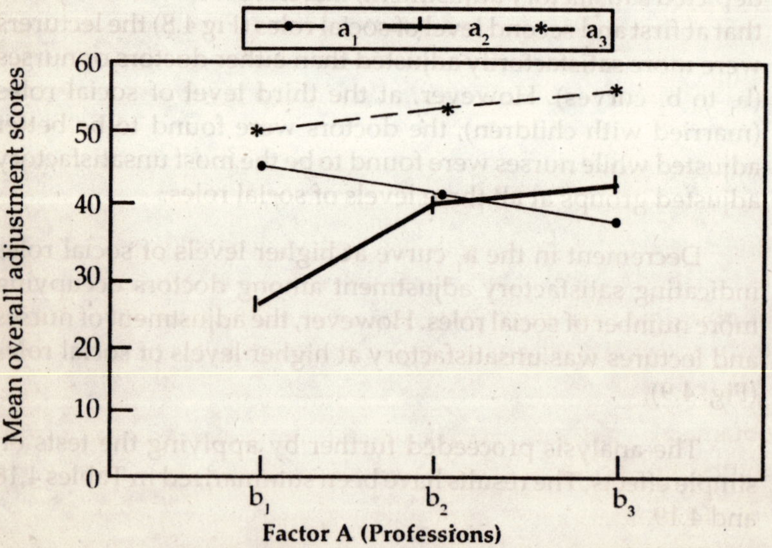

Fig. 4.9. A×B interaction profile (also profile of simple effects of factor B).

Table 4.18
Analysis of Variance for Simple Effects of A

Source of variance	*df*	*Sum of squares*	*Mean square*	*F*
A for b_1	2	7408.42	3704.211	14.88**
A for b_2	2	3205.09	1602.54	6.44**
A for b_3	2	4858.12	2429.06	9.76**
Within treatment (error)	261	64985.07	248.98	

** Significant at 0.01 level.

Table 4.19
Analysis of Variance for Simple Effects of B

Source of variance	*df*	*Sum of squares*	*Mean square*	*F*
B for a_1	2	518.06	259.03	1.04
B for a_2	2	3763.4	1881.7	7.56**
B for a_3	2	360.29	180.14	0.72
Within treatment (error)	261	64985.07	248.98	

** Significant at 0.01 level.

The statistical analysis in the above tables have been justified with the graphical interpretation of the different interaction between AB. F Value of Factor A have been found to be significant for each levels of Factors B which can further be observed from the curve representing simple effects of A for b_1, b_2 and b_3 having significant slopes. (Fig. 4.8).

Regarding simple effects of Factors B (Table 4.19) the obtained F values of Factor B for only a_2 level was found to be significant ($F=7.557, 2/261, p<0.01$).

This was followed by Newman Keuls test with the purpose of comparing the treatment means. The results have been summarized in Table 4.20 to 4.24.

Table 4.20

Schematic Summary of Results at b_1 Level (Unmarried)

a_2 *(Lecturers)*	a_2 *(Doctors)*	a_1 *(Nurses)*
28.1	42.87	49.87

Table 4.21

Schematic Summary of Results at b_2 Level (Married)

a_2 *(Lectures)*	a_1 *(Doctors)*	a_3 *(Nurses)*
39.3	40.23	52.4

Table 4.22

Schematic Summary of Results at b_3 Level (Married with Children)

a_1*(Doctors)*	a_1 *(Lecturers)*	a_3 *(Nurses)*
37.0	43.4	54.77

The above tables suggested that lecturers were significantly better adjusted than doctors and nurses at the first level of social roles. No significant difference however existed between doctors and lecturers at second and third levels of social roles. Nurses appeared to be comparatively unsatisfactorily adjusted at all levels. Comparison between treatment means at a_2 level has been given in following table.

Table 4.23

Schematic Summary of Results at a_2 Level (Lecturers)

b_1*(Unmarried)*	b_2 *(Married)*	b_3 *(Married with children)*
28.1	39.3	43.4

As evident, among the lecturers the unmarried were found to be significantly better adjusted than the married and those who were married and mother but the latter two groups were not found to differ significantly.

As the adult form of Bell's Adjustment Inventory provided five separate measures of personal and social adjustment, therefore, the adjustment of working women in each of these domains was analyzed by using same pattern of analyses.

For the first domain—the Home Adjustment, the summary of two way analysis of variance (ANOVA) has been presented in Table 4.24.

Table 4.24

Summary of Two Way Analysis of Variance for Home Adjustment

Source of variance	*df*	*Sum of squares*	*Mean square*	*F*
Between Factor A	2	316.14	158.07	7.82**
Between Factor B	2	219.16	109.58	5.42**
Interaction (A×B)	4	194.24	48.56	2.40
Within treatment	261	5274.53	20.21	

** Significant at 0.01 level.

It is evident from the Table 4.24 that while the F value of Factor A and Factor B were significant, that of interaction (F=2.403) did not exceed the critical value of 2.41 at .05 level and hence was not found to be significant.

Therefore, it can be concluded that while different professions and levels of social roles effected the home adjustment of working women independently, they did not show any interactive effect on the same.

Since the AB interaction was found to be significant no further tests on simple effects were applied.

Next, Health Adjustment of working women was assessed. The results of two-way analysis of variance have been summarized in Table 4.25.

While the obtained F valued of Factors B and the AB interaction were found to be significant, Factors A *i.e.,* professions did not seem to have any significant effect on the health adjustment (F=1.23, 2/261, p>.05). This was followed by tests on simple effect (Tables 4.26 and 4.27) and Newman Keuls test. But first the nature of interaction was studied by presenting geometrical representation of the outcome (Fig. 4.10 and Fig. 4.11).

Table 4.25

Summary of Two Way Analysis of Variance for Health Adjustment

Source of variance	*df*	*Sum of squares*	*Mean square*	*F*
Between Factor A	2	30.69	15.34	1.23
Between Factor B	2	299.29	149.64	12.03**
Interaction (A×B)	4	313.02	78.26	6.3**
Within treatment	261	3243.97	12.43	

** Significant at 0.01 level.

Table 4.26

Analysis of Variance for Simple Effects of A

Source of variance	*df*	*Sum of squares*	*Mean square*	*F*
A for b_1	2	154.15	77.08	6.20**
A for b_2	2	12.06	6.03	0.48
A for b_3	2	177.49	88.74	7.15**
Within treatment (error)	261	3243.97	12.43	

** Significant at 0.01 level.

Table 4.27

Analysis of Variance for Simple Effects of B

Source of variance	*df*	*Sum of squares*	*Mean square*	*F*
B for a_1	2	8.87	4.43	0.36
B for a_2	2	272.09	136.05	10.94**
B for a_3	2	331.35	165.68	13.33**
Within treatmet (error)	261	3243.97	12.43	

** Significant at 0.01 level.

Table revealed that observed valued of F in respect of simple effects of A for b_1 and b_3 were significant whereas, for the simple effects, of, F values were significant for a_2 (lectures) and a_3 (nurses) but not for a_1 (doctors).

Further, the comparisons were made among the treatment means as shown in Tables 4.28 to Table 4.31.

Table 4.28

Schematic Summary of Results at b_1 Level (Unmarried)

a_2 *(Lecturers)*	a_3 *(Nurses)*	a_1 *(Doctors)*
3.2	4.63	6.4

Table 4.29

Schematic Summary of Results at b_3 Level (Married with Children)

a_1 *(Doctors)*	a_2*(Lecturers)*	a_3*(Nurses)*
5.67	7.2	9.1

As in evident from the tables, at unmarried level of social roles, only the lectures and doctors were found to be significantly different with lecturers showing satisfactory health adjustment.

In case of married with children (Table 4.29), the doctors and nurses; nurses and lecturers were found to differ significantly. Doctors had more satisfactory health adjustment at this level. The following Tables (4.30 and 4.31) show the comparisons between treatment means at different levels of Factor A.

Table 4.30

Schematic Summary of Results at a_2 Level (Lecturers)

b_1 *(Unmarried)*	b_2*(Married)*	b_3*(Married with children)*
3.2	6.47	7.2

Table 4.31

Schematic Summary of Results at a_3 Level (Nurses)

b_1 *(Unmarried)*	b_2*(Married)*	b_3*(Married with children)*
4.63	5.6	9.1

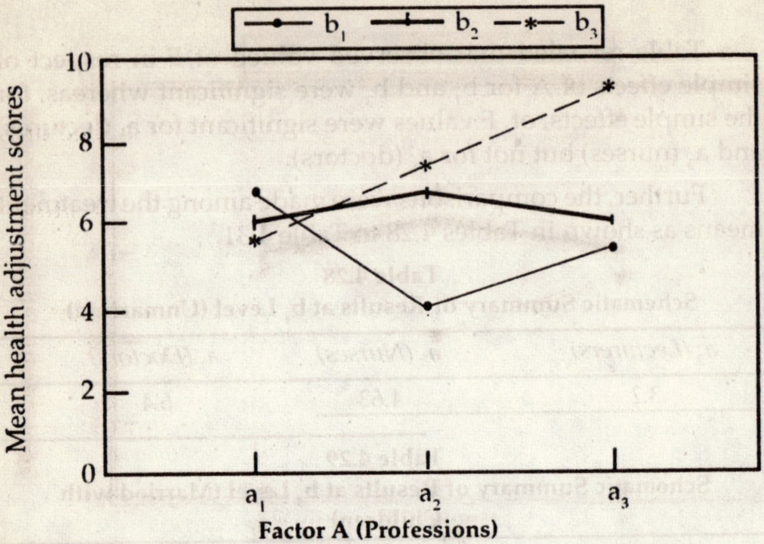

Fig. 4.10. A×B interaction profile (also profile of simple effects of factor A).

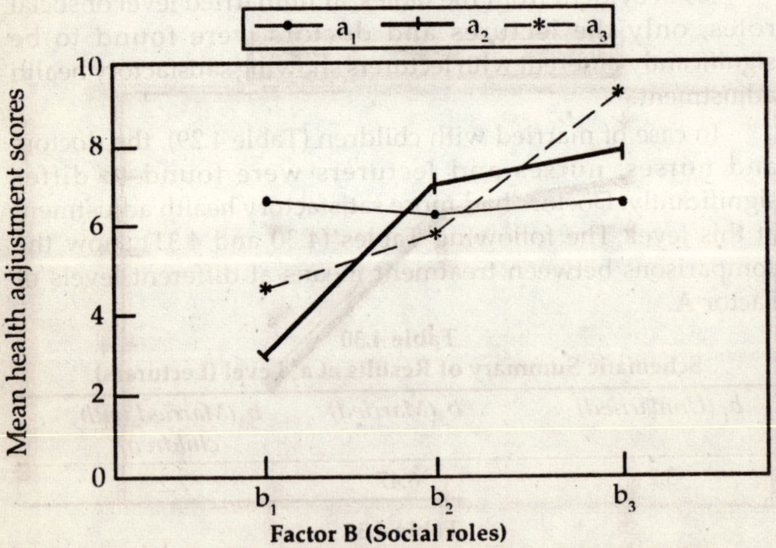

Fig. 4.11. A×B interaction profile (also profile of simple effects of factor B).

From the above tables it is clear that among the lecturers as well as nurses the unmarried group showed more satisfactory health adjustment.

As for the Social Adjustment, the results have been summarized in Table 4.32.

Table 4.32

Summary of Two Way Analysis of Variance for Social Adjustment

Source of variance	*df*	*Sum of squares*	*Mean square*	*F*
Between Factor A	2	997.65	498.83	22.46**
Between Factor B	2	95.14	47.57	2.14
Interaction (A×B)	4	149.21	37.30	1.68
Within treatment	261	5796.77	22.21	

** Significant at 0.01 level.

On the basis of results it can be interpreted that while different professions had significant effect on the social adjustment, the levels of social roles alone as well as in interaction with professions did not have any significant effect, therefore, no further tests were applied.

The independent as well as interactive effects of Factors A and B were further studied on Emotional Adjustment of working women (Table 4.33).

Table 4.33

Summary of Two Way Analysis of Variance for Emotional Adjustment

Source of variance	*df*	*Sum of squares*	*Mean square*	*F*
Between Factor A	2	825.83	412.91	13.99**
Between Factor B	2	24.23	12.11	0.41
Interaction (A×B)	4	669.10	167.28	5.67**
Within treatment	264	7701	29.50	

** Significant at 0.01 level.

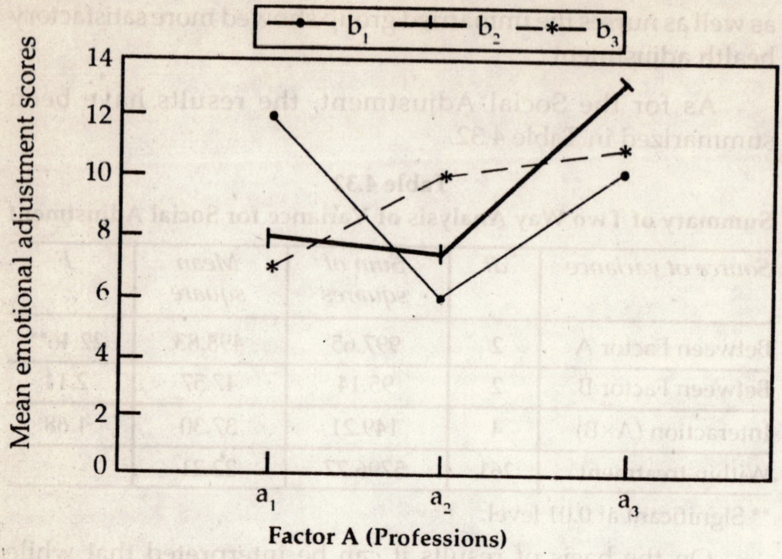

Fig. 4.12. A×B interaction profile (also profile of simple effects of factor A).

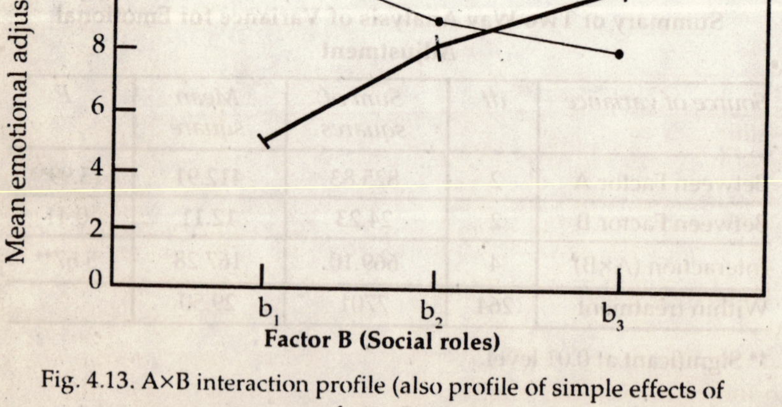

Fig. 4.13. A×B interaction profile (also profile of simple effects of factor B).

The above table revealed that while F-values for Factor A and AB interaction were significant that of Factor B was not significant, indicating no significant effect of number of social roles on emotional adjustment. Fig. 4.12 and 4.13 depict the nature of this interaction.

Because of significant AB interaction, tests on simple effects were applied results of which have been in Tables 4.34 and 4.35.

Table 4.34

Analysis of Variance for Simple Effects of A

Source of variance	*df*	*Sum of squares*	*Mean square*	*F*
A for b_1	2	622.15	311.08	10.54**
A for b_2	2	593.68	296.84	10.06**
A for b_3	2	279.09	139.54	4.73**
Within treatment (error)	261	7701	29.50	

** Significant at 0.01 level.

Table 4.35

Analysis of Variance for Simple Effects of B

Source of variance	*df*	*Sum of squares*	*Mean square*	*F*
B for a_1	2	262.86	131.43	4.45*
B for a_2	2	308.62	154.31	5.23**
B for a_3	2	121.62	60.81	2.06
Within treatment (error)	261	7701	29.50	

** Significant at 0.01 level.

From the table of simple effects of A, it can be observed that obtained F value of Factor A (Professions) were significant at all the levels of Factor B (Social Roles) at .01 level. As for the simple effects of Factor B, F values for only a_1 and a_1 levels were found to significant. These results have been justified with the graphical interpretation of interaction between A and B as shown in Fig. 4.12 and 4.13.

More specific comparisons among the treatment means were made by using Newman Keuls test. Summary of results has been given in Tables 4.36 to 4.40.

Table 4.36
Schematic Summary of Results at b_1 Level (Unmarried)

a_2 *(Lecturers)*	a_3 *(Nurses)*	a_1 *(Doctors)*
5.5	10.87	11.26

Table 4.37
Schematic Summary of Results at b_2 Level (Married)

a_2 *(Lecturers)*	a_1 *(Doctors)*	a_1 *(Nurses)*
7.9	8.37	13.57

Table 4.38
Schematic Summary of Results at b_3 Level (Married with Children)

a_1 *(Doctors)*	a_3 *(Lecturers)*	a_1 *(Nurses)*
7.2	10.03	11.43

At b_1 level (unmarried) the lecturers were found to be significantly better adjusted emotionally than nurses and doctors. No significant difference was observed between nurses and doctors at this level of social role.

Comparison between treatment means at b_2 level (married) suggested that nurses had significantly unsatisfactory emotional adjustment than doctors and lecturers while no significant difference existed between lecturers and doctors at this level.

At the b_3 level (married with children) doctors were found to be significantly better emotionally adjusted than either lecturers or the nurses (Table 4.38).

In additions to this, simple effects of B for a_1 and a_2 levels were studied, the results of which have been presented in Tables 4.39 and 4.40.

Table 4.39
Schematic Summary of Results at a_1 Level (Doctors)

b_3 (mMarried with children)	b_2 (Married)	b_1 (Unmarried)
7.2	8.37	11.26

Table 4.40
Schematic Summary of Results at a_2 Level (Lecturers)

b_1 (Unmarried)	b_2 (Married)	b_3 (Married with children)
5.5	7.9	10.03

As evident from the tables, the among the doctors, those who were married and having children were significantly better adjusted emotionally that those holding fewer social roles. However, no significant difference was obtained between doctors who were married and those who were mothers as well. In case of lecturers, no significant difference was found between unmarried and married and also between married and those who were mothers.

In nutshell, while at unmarried (1) and married (2) social role level the lecturers were found to be better emotionally adjusted, doctors showed better emotional adjustment at the third level of social role, *i.e.* married with children (3). Among doctors those who were married and mother were better emotionally adjusted whereas in lecturers the unmarried group was found to be more emotionally stable than other groups.

The Occupational Adjustment of working women was then studied and the summary of the results as shown in Table 4.41 reflected that while F value for Factor A and AB interaction were significant, that for Factor B was no significant.

In light of the results presented in Table 4.41, it can be concluded that while the occupational adjustment was significantly affected by different professions and their interaction with different levels of social roles, no such effect

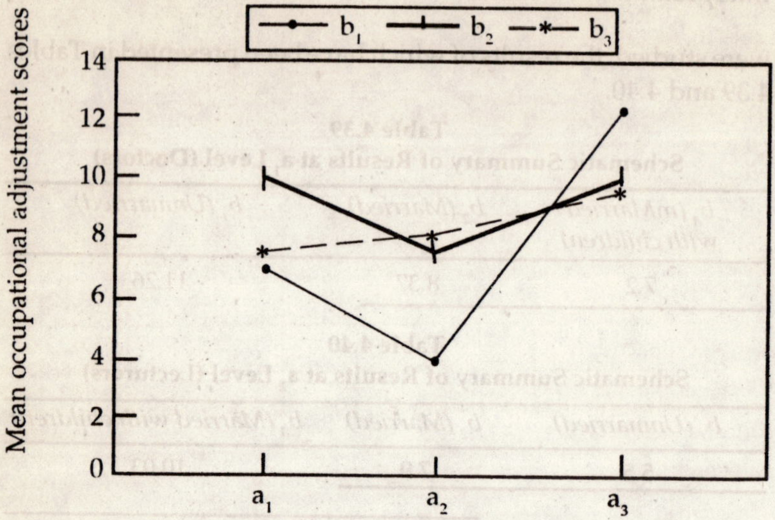

Fig. 4.14. A×B interaction profile (also profile of simple effects of factor A).

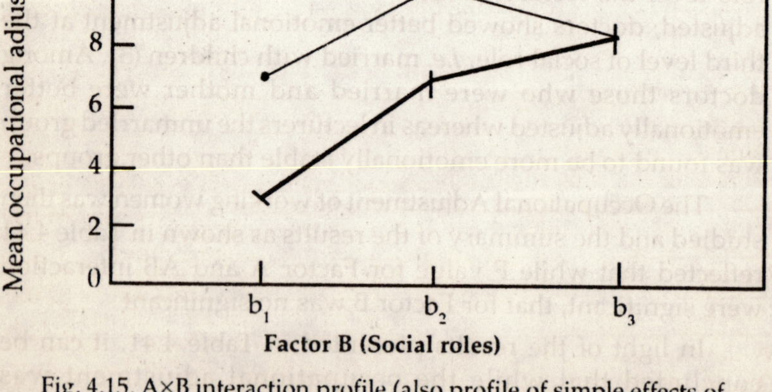

Fig. 4.15. A×B interaction profile (also profile of simple effects of factor B).

could be found for social roles when taken alone. Fig 4.14 and 4.15 further depict the nature of the AB interaction.

The way ANOVA was followed by tests on simple effects, the results of which have been given in Tables. 4.42 and 4.43.

Table 4.41

Summary of Two Way Analysis of Variance for Occupational Adjustment

Source of variance	*df*	*Sum of squares*	*Mean square*	*F*
Between Factor A	2	837.42	418.71	19.41**
Between Factor B	2	72.8	36.4	1.69
Interaction (A×B)	4	437.11	109.28	5.06**
Within Treatment	261	5631.33	21.58	

** Significant at 0.01 level.

Table 4.42

Analysis of Variance for Simple Effects of A

Source of variance	*df*	*Sum of squares*	*Mean square*	*F*
A for b_1	2	1076.15	538.07	24.94**
A for b_2	2	128.62	64.31	2.98
A for b_3	2	69.75	34.88	1.62
Within treatment (error)	261	5631.33	21.58	

** Significant at 0.01 level.

Table 4.43

Analysis of Variance for Simple Effects of B

Source of variance	*df*	*Sum of squares*	*Mean square*	*F*
B for a_1	2	108.20	54.10	2.51
B for a_2	2	277.62	138.81	6.43**
B for a_3	2	124.09	62.04	2.88
Within treatment (error)	261	5631.33	21.58	

** Significant at 0.01 level.

As apparent from above tables, simple effect of A for only b_1 level was found to be significant whereas for Factor B, obtained F value of 6.43 for a_2 level was significant.

The comparison between the treatment means were then made at b_1 and a_2 levels to know exactly which of the three groups differed significantly. The results have been presented in Tables 4.44 and 4.45.

Table 4.44

Schematic Summary of Results at b_1 Level (Unmarried)

a_2 *(Lecturers)*	a_1 *(Doctors)*	a_3 *(Nurses)*
3.63	7.17	12.07

Table 4.45

Schematic Summary of Results at a_2 Level (Lecturers)

b_1 *(Unmarried)*	b_2 *(Married)*	b_3 *(Married with children)*
3.63	7.2	7.5

Above tables make it clear that when the number of social roles was minimum (unmarried in this case), all the professionals differed significantly from each other and the lecturers were found to have more satisfactory adjustment with regard to their occupation. Within the lecturers, the married were found to have more satisfactory occupational adjustment as compared to those occupying other two levels of social roles.

To be more precise, it was observed that lecturers were betters adjusted (overall) and emotionally at unmarried and married social role level while in case of married and having children doctors showed better overall adjustment, health adjustment and emotional adjustment than the lecturers or nurses. Among the lecturers, occupational adjustment was found to be better in unmarried group as compared to those at other two levels of social roles.

So, the fourth hypothesis stating that the number of social roles would significantly effect the level of adjustment in different domains (home, health, social, emotional, occupational) has been partially proved. The only study reviewed in this context was by Bawa and Singh (1996) in which the professional groups taken were nurses, teachers and clerks. The results revealed nurses to be better adjusted on home, emotional and occupational domains while teachers and better health and social adjustment. On the contrary, nurses were found to be unsatisfactorily adjusted that doctors or lecturers in the present study. Not even a single study reviewed measured various domains of adjustment in relations to different professions as well as social roles of working women and here underlies the novelty of the present research.

Lastly, the Quality of Life of working women was studied in relation to the same independent variables. The two-way analysis of variance (Table 4.46) showed significant effect of professions and social roles but no such effect of their interaction on the overall quality of life. Hence, no test on simple effects was further applied.

Table 4.46

Summary of Two Way Analysis of Variance for Quality of Life

Source of variance	*df*	*Sum of squares*	*Mean square*	*F*
Between Factor A (Professions)	2	6.90	3.45	6.39**
Between Factor B (Social roles)	2	9.36	4.68	8.66**
Interaction (A×B)	4	4.68	1.17	2.17
Within treatment	261	139.97	0.54	

** Significant at 0.01 level.

As the WHO quality of life-BREF measured quality of life in four domains (physical health, psychological, social relationships, environmental). Therefore, the scores in each of these domains were statistically analyzed by applying two-way analysis of variance (ANOVA), followed by tests on simple effects and New Man Keuls test. But, first a single item related to general health was assessed separately. The summary of two-

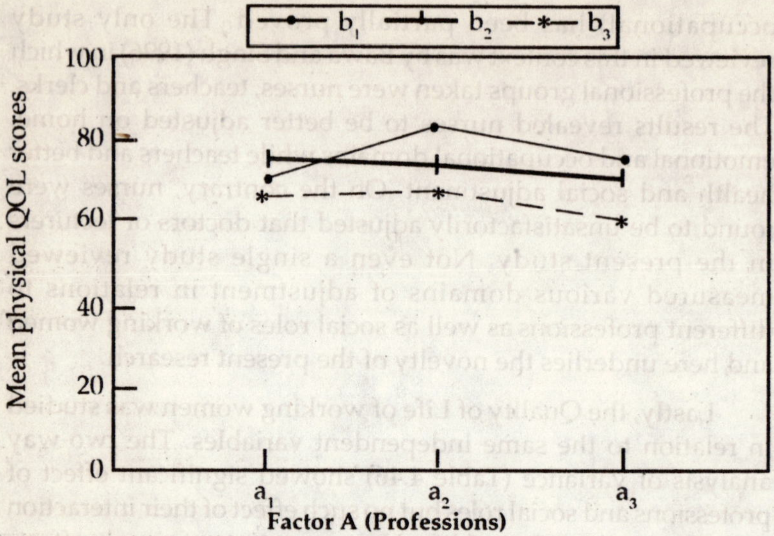

Fig. 4.16. A×B interaction profile (also profile of simple effects of factor A).

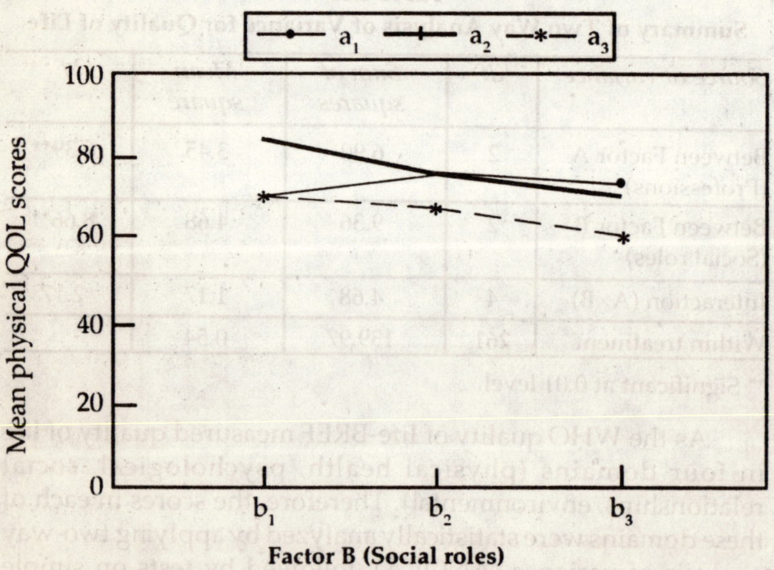

Fig. 4.17. A×B interaction profile (also profile of simple effects of factor B).

way analysis of variance presented in Table 4.47 suggested that just in as overall quality of life, Factor A and Factor B were found to significantly effect the general health of working women but no such effect was apparent in case of their interaction. Again, due to insignificant F value for interaction, no further tests were applied.

Table 4.47

Summary of Two Way Analysis of Variance for General Health

Source of variance	*df*	*Sum of squares*	*Mean square*	*F*
Between Factor A (Professions)	2	4.87	2.43	4.56*
Between Factor B (Social roles)	2	16.47	8.23	15.42**
Interaction (A×B)	4	2.13	0.53	1.00
Within treatment	261	139.4	0.53	

** Significant at 0.01 level.

Regarding the physical quality of life the results shown in Table 4.48 revealed that Factor A ($F=14.760$, 2/261, $p<0.01$), Factor B ($F=17.059$, 2/261, $p<0.01$) and AB interaction ($F=3.456$, 4/261, $p<0.01$) has significant effect. The graphical representation Fig. 4.16 and 4.17 further depict the nature of this interaction.

Table 4.48

Summary of Two Way Analysis of Variance for Physical QOL

Source of variance	*df*	*Sum of squares*	*Mean square*	*F*
Between Factor A (Professions)	2	4564.15	2282.07	14.73**
Between Factor B (Social roles)	2	5306.49	2653.24	17.13**
Interaction (A×B)	4	2175.92	543.98	3.5**
Within treatment	261	40434.7	154.92	

** Significant at 0.01 level.

Since the AB interaction was found to be significant, the tests on simple effects (Table 4.49 and 4.50) followed by New Man Keuls test (Table 4.51 to 4.55) were applied.

Table 4.49
Analysis of Variance for Simple Effects of A

Source of variance	*df*	*Sum of squares*	*Mean square*	*F*
A for b_1	2	3589.30	1794.65	11.58**
A for b_2	2	1040.67	520.33	3.36*
A for b_3	2	2107.98	1053.99	6.80**
Within treatment (error)	261	40434.72	154.92	

* Significant at 0.05 level.
** Significant at 0.01 level.

Table 4.50
Analysis of Variance for Simple Effects of B

Source of variance	*df*	*Sum of squares*	*Mean square*	*F*
B for a_1	2	742.32	371.16	2.39
B for a_2	2	4323.66	2161.83	13.95**
B for a_3	2	2626.98	1313.49	8.48**
Within treatment (error)	261	40434.72	154.92	

** Significant at 0.01 level.

As evident, the observed values of F in respect of simple effect of A for levels b_1, b_2 and b_3 were found to be significant whereas simple effects of B of levels a_2 and a_3 were significant.

The comparisons between treatment meant at the levels found to be significant in Table 4.49 and 4.50 have been presented in the tables below.

Table 4.51
Schematic Summary of Results at b_1 Level (Unmarried)

a_3 *(Nurses)*	a_1 *(Doctors)*	a_2 *(Lecturers)*
70.59	70.95	84.17

Table 4.52
Schematic Summary of Results at b_2 Level (Married)

a_3 *(Nurses)*	a_2 *(Lecturers)*	a_1 *(Doctors)*
68.45	75.36	75.95

Table 4.53
Schematic Summary of Results at b_3 Level (Married with Children)

a_3 *(Nurses)*	a_2 *(Lecturers)*	a_1 *(Doctors)*
58.21	67.62	69.17

Table 4.54
Schematic Summary of Results at a_2 Level (Lecturers)

b_3 *(Married with children)*	b_2 *(Married)*	b_1 *(Unmarried)*
67.19	75.36	84.17

Table 4.55
Schematic Summary of Results at a_3 Level (Nurses)

b_3 *(Married with children)*	b_2 *(Married)*	b_1 *(Unmarried)*
58.21	68.45	70.59

At the unmarried level, the lecturers were found to have significantly better physical QOL while doctors faired better at the other two levels of social roles. Among lecturers and nurses those married and having children had poor physical quality of life.

Psychological QOL of working women was then assessed. The summary of two way analysis of variance has been given

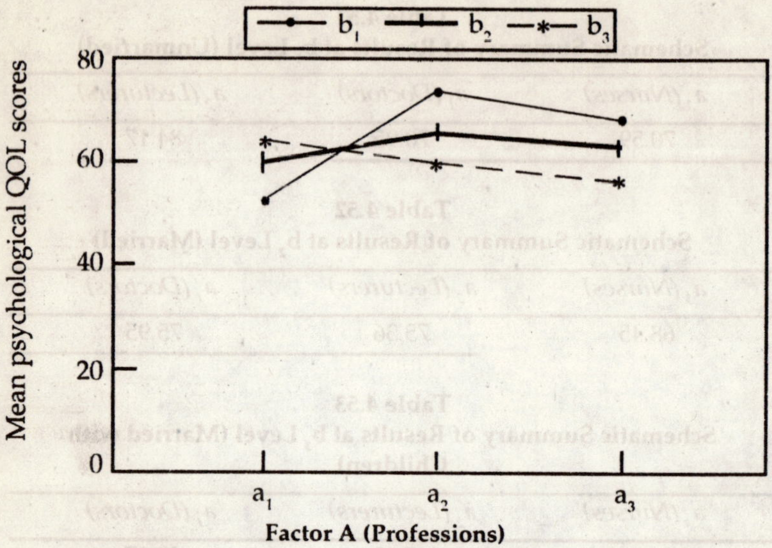

Fig. 4.18. A×B interaction profile (also profile of simple effects of factor A).

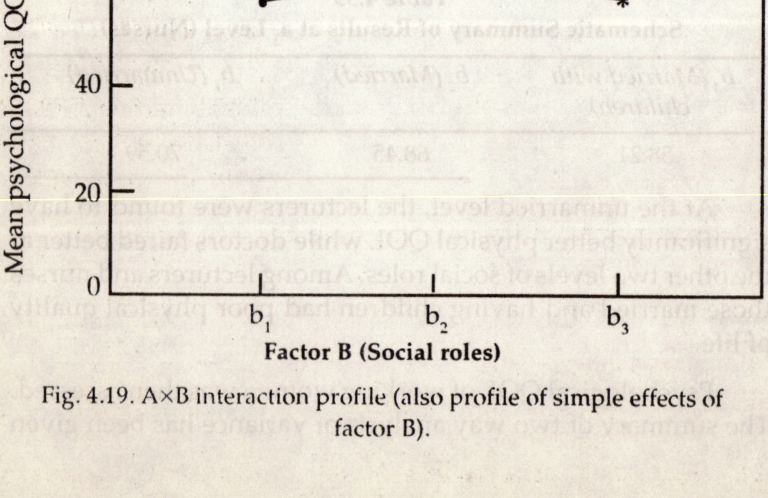

Fig. 4.19. A×B interaction profile (also profile of simple effects of factor B).

in Table 4.56. Results revealed that while Factor A independently as well as in interaction with Factor B had significant effects, Factor B ($F=1.98$, 2/261, $p>0.05$) when taken alone was not significant. The nature of AB interaction can further be observed from its geometrical representation (Fig. 4.18 and 4.19).

Table 4.56

Summary of Two Way Analysis of Variance for Psychological QOL

Source of variance	*df*	*Sum of squares*	*Mean square*	*F*
Between Factor A (Professions)	2	3590.41	1795.20	9.77**
Between Factor B (Social roles)	2	728.91	364.45	1.98
Interaction (A×B)	4	4602.49	1150.62	6.26**
Within treatment	261	47938.08	183.67	

** Significant at 0.01 level.

This was followed by tests on simple effects of A and B, results of which have been summarized in Tables 4.57 and 4.58. The calculated values of F in respect of simple effect of A for levels b_1 (unmarried) and b_3 (married and having children) were found to significant. For Factor B, the F values were significant at all the levels of Factor A.

Table 4.57

Analysis of Variance for Simple Effects of A

Source of variance	*df*	*Sum of squares*	*Mean square*	*F*
A for b_1	3	5987.34	2993.67	16.30**
A for b_2	2	964.13	482.06	2.62
A for b_3	2	1240.74	620.37	3.38*
Within treatment (error)	261	47938.08	183.67	

** Significant at 0.01 level.

Table 4.58
Analysis of Variance for Simple Effects of B

Source of variance	*df*	*Sum of squares*	*Mean square*	*F*
B for a_1	2	1731.86	865.93	4.71**
B for a_2	2	2045.13	1022.57	5.57**
B for a_3	2	1553.62	776.81	4.23*
Within treatment (error)	261	47938.08	183.67	

** Significant at 0.01 level.

Comparison between treatment means using the New Man Keuls procedure (Table 4.59 to 4.63) indicated that at b_1 levels all the professionals were significantly different from each other as also presented graphically in Fig 4.18 (curve representing b_1). Lecturers were having better psychological QOL at this level. Only nurses and doctors were found to be significantly different at the b_3 level with doctors (a_1) displaying better psychological QOL.

Table 4.59
Schematic Summary of Results at b_1 Level (Unmarried)

a_1 (Doctors)	*a_3 (Nurses)*	*a_2 (Lecturers)*
55.69	67.5	75.56

Table 4.60
Schematic Summary of Results at b_3 Level (Married with Children)

a_3 (Nurses)	*a_2 (Lecturers)*	*a_1 (Doctors)*
57.36	63.89	66.11

Table 4.61
Schematic Summary of Results at a_1 Level (Doctors)

b_1 (Unmarried)	*b_2 (Married)*	*b_3 (Married with children)*
55.69	63.19	66.11

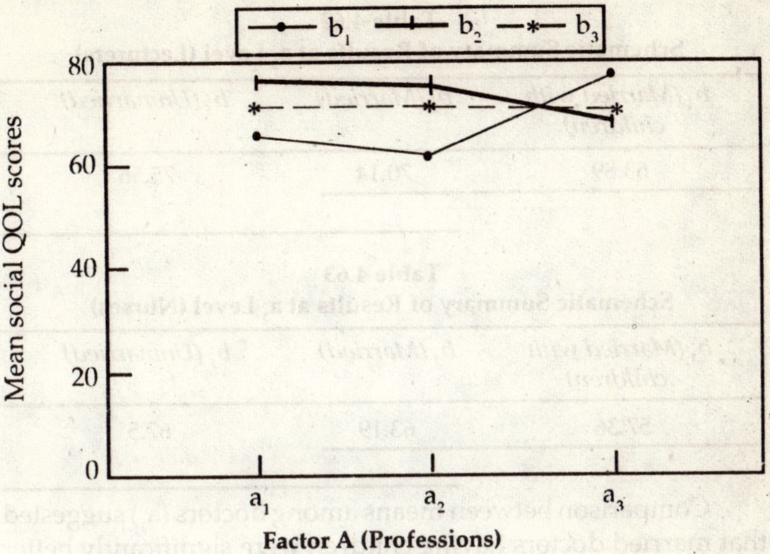

Fig. 4.20. A×B interaction profile (also profile of simple effects of factor A).

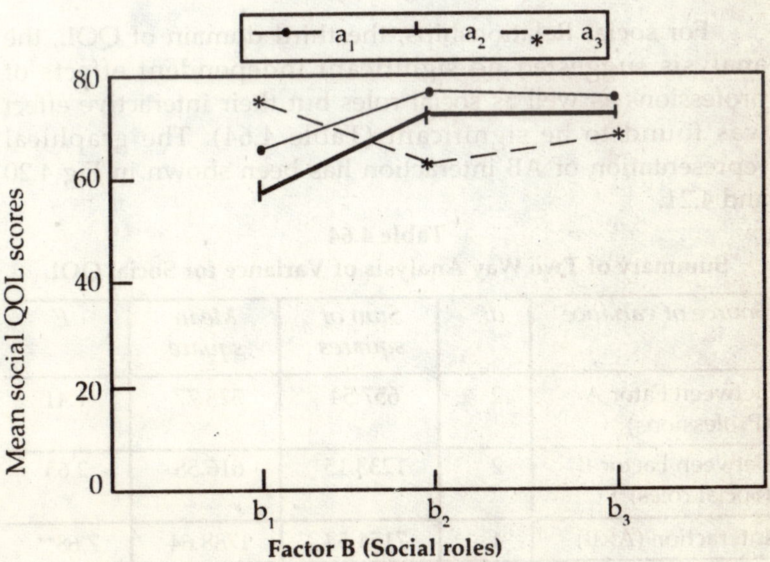

Fig. 4.21. A×B interaction profile (also profile of simple effects of factor B).

Table 4.62
Schematic Summary of Results at a_2 Level (Lecturers)

b_3 *(Married with children)*	b_2 *(Married)*	b_1 *(Unmarried)*
63.89	70.14	75.56

Table 4.63
Schematic Summary of Results at a_3 Level (Nurses)

b_3 *(Married with children)*	b_2 *(Married)*	b_1 *(Unmarried)*
57.36	63.19	67.5

Comparison between means among doctors (a_1) suggested that married doctors having children were significantly better than the unmarried ones. Whereas in case of both lecturers (a_2) and nurses (a_3), the women who were married showed significantly better psychological quality of life.

For social Relationships, the third domain of QOL, the analysis suggested no significant independent effects of professions as well as social roles but their interactive effect was found to be significant (Table 4.64). The graphical representation of AB interaction has been shown in Fig 4.20 and 4.21.

Table 4.64
Summary of Two Way Analysis of Variance for Social QOL

Source of variance	*df*	*Sum of squares*	*Mean square*	*F*
Between Fator A (Professions)	2	657.54	328.77	1.41
Between Factor B (Social roles)	2	1233.15	616.58	2.65
Interaction (A×B)	4	7154.58	1788.64	7.68**
Within treatment	261	60808.45	232.98	

** Significant at 0.01 level.

The tests on simple effects further indicated that obtained F values of A for b_1 and b_2 and B for all levels of A were significant (Tables 4.65 and 4.66).

Comparisons between treatment means were than made at those levels of Factors A and B which were found to be significant. The results have been presented in Tables 4.67 to 4.71.

Table 4.65

Analysis of Variance for Simple Effects of A

Source of variance	*df*	*Sum of squares*	*Mean square*	*F*
A for b_1	2	4003.47	2001.73	8.59**
A for b_2	2	3223.79	1611.90	6.92**
A for b_3	2	584.86	292.43	1.26
Within treatment (error)	261	60808.45	232.98	

** Significant at 0.01 level.

Table 4.66

Analysis of Variance for Simple Effects of B

Source of variance	*df*	*Sum of squares*	*Mean square*	*F*
B for a_1	2	1857.99	928.99	3.99*
B for a_2	2	4168.21	2084.11	8.95**
B for a_3	2	2361.53	1180.77	5.07**
Within treatment (error)	261	60808.45	232.98	

** Significant at 0.01 level.

Table 4.67

Schematic Summary of Results at b_1 Level (Unmarried)

a_2 *(Lecturers)*	a_1 *(Doctors)*	a_3 *(Nurses)*
59.17	65.83	75.42

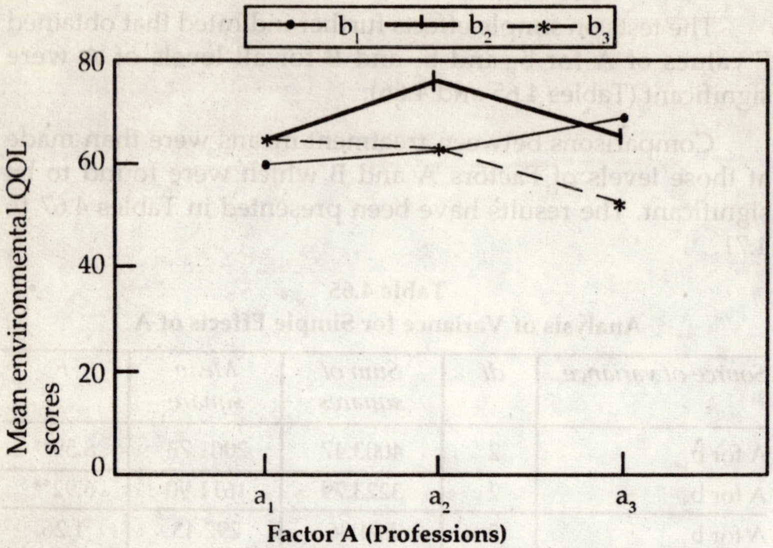

Fig. 4.22. A×B interaction profile (also profile of simple effects of factor A).

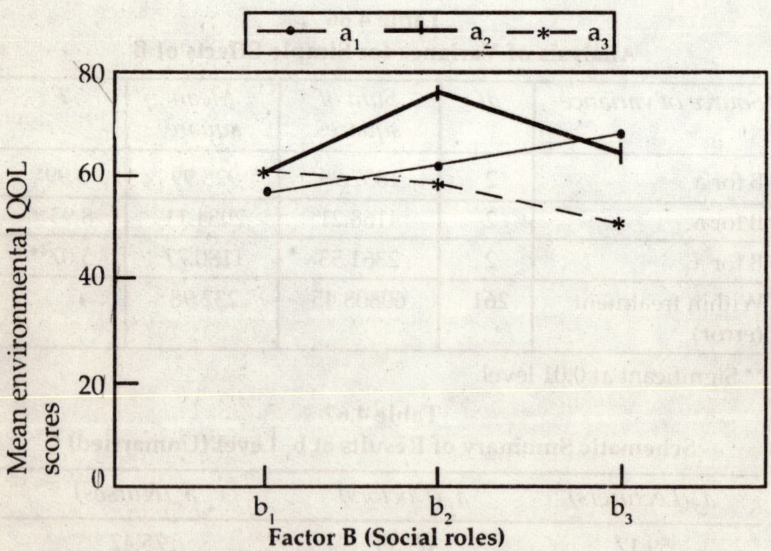

Fig. 4.23. A×B interaction profile (also profile of simple effects of factor B).

Table 4.68
Schematic Summary of Results at b_2 Level (Married)

a_3 *(Nurses)*	a_2 *(Lecturers)*	a_1 *(Doctors)*
63.61	75.56	76.49

Table 4.69
Schematic Summary of Results at a_1 Level (Doctors)

b_1 *(Unmarried)*	b_3 *(Married with children)*	b_2 *(Married)*
65.83	71.94	76.94

Table 4.70
Schematic Summary of Results at a_2 Level (Lecturers)

b_1 *(Unmarried)*	b_3 *(Married with children)*	b_2 *(Married)*
59.17	70.00	75.56

Table 4.71
Schematic Summary of Results at a_3 Level (Nurses)

b_2 *(Married)*	b_3 *(Married with children)*	b_1 *(Unmarried)*
63.61	65.83	75.42

At b_1 level, nurses were found to be significantly better in social relationship front whereas at b_2 level doctors displayed better QOL with regard to social relationship. The comparison between means at levels of A suggested married doctors to be better than the ones occupying other two social roles. Among the lecturers, again married were found to be significantly better than unmarried whereas in case of nurses unmarried showed better social relationship QOL. No significant differences was observed between married and married with children.

QOL of working women in environment domain was found to be significantly affected by professions, social roles as well as their interaction (Table 4.72).

Table 4.72
Summary of Two Way Analysis of Variance for Environmental QOL

Source of variance	*df*	*Sum of squares*	*Mean square*	*F*
Between Factor A (Professions)	2	3312.14	1656.07	7.90**
Between Factor B (Social roles)	2	2483.14	1241.57	5.92**
Interaction (A×B)	4	3192.42	798.10	3.81**
Within treatment	261	54707.36	209.61	

** Significant at 0.01 level.

Nature of AB interaction was further explored by its graphical representation as is shown in Fig. 4.22 and 4.23. Moreover, tests on simple effects (Table 4.73 and 4.74) indicated that F values of Factor A for b_2 and b_3 and Factor B for a_2 and a_3 were significant.

Table 4.73
Summary of Analysis of Variance for Simple Effects of A

Source of variance	*df*	*Sum of squares*	*Mean square*	*F*
A for b_1	2	87.46	43.73	0.21
A for b_2	2	3720.27	1860.14	8.87**
A for b_3	2	2696.84	1348.42	6.43**
Within treatmnet (error)	261	54707.36	209.61	

** Significant at 0.01 level.

Table 4.74
Summary of Analysis of Variance for Simple Effects of B

Source of variance	*df*	*Sum of squares*	*Mean square*	*F*
B for a_1	2	325.74	162.87	0.78
B for a_2	2	3529.30	1764.65	8.42**
B for a_3	2	1820.52	910.26	4.34*
Within treatment (error)	261	54707.36	209.61	

** Significant at 0.01 level.

The summary of comparisons between treatment means at these levels have been shown in Tables 4.75 to 4.78.

Table 4.75

Schematic Summary of Results at b_2 Level (Married)

a_1 *(Doctors)*	a_3 *(Nurses)*	a_2 *(Lecturers)*
61.46	64.48	76.35

Table 4.76

Schematic Summary of Results at b_3 Level (Married with Children)

a_3 *(Nurses)*	a_2 *(Lecturers)*	a_1 *(Doctors)*
52.60	63.23	65.00

Table 4.77

Schematic Summary of Results at a_2 Level (Lecturers)

b_1 *(Unmarried)*	b_3 *(Married with children)*	b_2 *(Married)*
62.92	63.23	76.35

Table 4.78

Schematic Summary of Results at a_3 Level (Nurses)

b_3 *(Married with children)*	b_2 *(Married)*	b_1 *(Unmarried)*
52.60	61.46	62.71

To put in words, while at married social roles levels, the lecturers showed significantly better environmental QOL than other two groups of professionals, the doctors faired better at the third level of social roles. Focus on the lecturers suggested married lecturers to be significantly better than those at other two levels of social roles (Table 4.77). Among nurses, the unmarried and married were found to be significantly different from those who were married and having children.

In this way the fifth hypothesis stating that multiple social roles of working women would have varied effect on different domains of QOL (physical, psychological, social and environment) has been proved by the present findings. Since, the assessment of QOL of working women in different domains in relation to their professions and social roles is the first attempt therefore, no study in support or contradiction to the present research could be presented.

The results also revealed that the role conflict, self esteem, levels of adjustment and quality of life of working women differed significantly in relation to their professions. Moreover, the professions and social roles were found to have interactive effect on these dependent variables hence supporting the sixth and seventh hypothesis. The present results are in line with Haworth (1997) who reported valued position in work to have important association with positive psychological states.

After studying the interactive effect of professions and social (familial) roles, Stepwise Multiple Regression Analysis was employed to assess the contribution of five variable, *i.e.* roles conflict, self esteem, adjustment, duty hours and levels of social roles on the overall quality of life of the working women.

The derived equation has been described below :

While predicting the overall QOL only the role conflict, adjustment and levels of social roles were found to be significant predictors. They together explained only 19% of variance [$R^3 \times 100$, (R=.440)] and were significant (f=21.252, 3/266, p<.000).

The derived equation of QOL can be stated as under in symbolic and score form.

$$\overline{X}_{QOL} = b(\overline{X}_{RC}) + b(\overline{X}_{ADJ}) + b(\overline{X}_{LEV}) + K$$

$$4.02 = (-.00818 \times 74.02) + (\mathbf{-.0125^{*} \times 43.10}) + (-.159 \times 2) + 5.483$$

(*The highlighted scores of adjustment in the present equation predicting QOL as well as in further equations for different domains of QOL actually indicate the direct relationship since the pattern of scoring for adjustment was inverse with low scores depicting satisfactory adjustment.)

Role conflict and levels of social roles were detected as the significant negative predictors as their obtained value of significance was 0.01 and 0.003 respectively. The levels of social roles would decrease about 8% of the total quality of life. If the role of adjustment and levels of social roles are partialled out, the correlation between role conflict and QOL was -0.151. As for the levels of social roles and QOL, the correlation was -0.18.

The quality of life (physical, psychological, social relationships, environmental) of professionals was then predicted on the basis of nine predictors comprising five measures of adjustment (Home, Health, Social, Emotional and Occupational), the role conflict, self esteem, duty hours as well as different levels of social roles.

For the physical QOL it was found that out of nine, only role conflict, health adjustment, level of social roles and social adjustment turned out to be significant predictors. They together explained only 28% of variance [$R^2 \times 100$, (R=.53)] and were significant (F=26.06, 4/265, p<.0000).

The derived equation for physical QOL has been given below :

$$\overline{X}_{Phy \bullet QOL} = b(\overline{X}_{RC}) + b(\overline{X}_{HE \bullet ADJ}) + b(\overline{X}_{LEV}) + (\overline{X}_{SO \bullet ADJ}) + K$$

71.1=(-.290 × 74.02) + **(-.662 × 6.01)** + (-.3.21 × 2) + **(-.41 × 12.45)** × 108.136

The equation revealed that in predicting physical QOL, role conflict and level of social roles contributed negatively as their obtained value of significance was .000 and .0007 respectively. In case of health and social adjustment, the negative values were dude to the inverse scoring pattern. Hence to interpret it simply, both contributed positively towards Physical QOL.

While predicting the psychological QOL, again only 4 out of 9 variables, *i.e.* self esteem, duty hours, home adjustment and levels of social rules were found to be significant predictors. It was found that they together explained only 25% of variance [R_2x100, R(=.495)] and were significant (F=21.547, 4/265, p<.000). While self esteem alone accounted for 14% of variance, duty hours explained 7% of variance, home adjustment and levels of social roles explained only 2% of variance each.

The derived equation for psychological QOL has been give below :

$$\overline{X}_{Psy \bullet QOL} = b(\overline{X}_{SE}) + b(\overline{X}_{DH}) + b(\overline{X}_{HO \bullet ADJ}) + b(\overline{X}_{LEV}) + K$$

64.7 = (.342 × 66.07) + (-1.85 × 7.33) + **(-.435 × 6.85)** + (-2.03 × 2) + 62.78

The equation revealed that in predicting psychological QOL, duty hours and levels of social roles contributed negatively whereas self esteem as well as home adjustment were found to contribute positively.

In predicting social relationships QOL, only three factors *i.e.* self esteem, occupational adjustment and social adjustment were found to be significant predictors. Self esteem was observed to be better predictor of social relationship QOL. Together they explained only 9.4% variance [R^2 x 100, (R=.306)] were significant (F=9.176, 3/266, p<.000).

The derived equation for social relationship QOL can be stated as under in symbolic and score form :

$$\overline{X}_{(Soc.R \bullet QOL)} = b(\overline{X}_{SE}) + b(\overline{X}_{OCC \bullet ADJ}) + b(\overline{X}_{SO \bullet ADJ}) + K$$

69.36 = (.247 × 66.07) + (.693 × 8.22) + **(-.461 × 12.45)** + 53.1

The equation revealed that in predicting social relationship QOL while self esteem and social adjustment were found to be contributing positively, occupational adjustment (because of inverse pattern of scoring) contributed negatively.

While predicting environmental QOL only self esteem and role conflict emerged as a significant contributors, together explaining 14% of variance [R^2 x 100, (R=.373)] were significant (F=21.557, 2/267, p<.000).

The derived equation for Environmental QOL has been presented below :

$$\overline{X}_{Env \bullet QOL} = b(\overline{X}_{SE}) = (\overline{X}_{RC}) + K$$

63.27 =(.264 × 66.07) + (-.188 × 74.02) + 59.762

The equation revealed that in predicting environmental QOL self esteem contributed positively as its obtained value of significance was .000 whereas the role conflict contributed negatively.

An attempt to predict QOL of working women on the basis of nine predictors hence revealed their significance but little contribution. It attests to the view that the Quality of Life is the product of number of variables and these variables may be only few of them.

5 EVALUATION OF PSYCHOLOGICAL CONSEQUENCES OF MULTIPLE ROLES JUGGLING

The trend in the labour force participation indicates that in the years ahead, the greatest addition in the work force will be of women in the age group of 24 to 54 years. That means more and more women will be adding on a new role to their traditional role of a homemaker. Therefore, a need was felt to evaluate the psychological effects of multiple role juggling in working women. The present study proceeded on the lines of the question raised by Gilbert (1984) : "Can a concept of a career that includes involvement in the family and the occupational roles realistically coexist with institutions that embody the value of a patriarchal society?" In trying to find an answer to this question the present chapter will probe into psychological consequences in relation to social (familial) roles of women and their profession. The directions for future studies shall also be proposed in the later section of this chapter.

In the first phase of the study results suggested working women to have higher self esteem than their non working counterparts. This may be due to the fact that a husband's income is the only reward a housewife can share, since she can actually possess this reward and use this to engage in certain behaviours (*i.e.* making consumer purchases) which increase her status among peers. All other rewards (or successes) tend to reflect indirectly on the wife (for having a desirable or successful husband). Indeed this dependence on her husband for success may reduce her feelings of worth, especially if she is well educated and, presumably, able to earn her own rewards. This powerlessness may reduce her sense of competence in dealing with the life situations, which is an important dimension of self esteem. Thus, the relative lack of independent achievement may lower a housewife's self esteem. Therefore, while she may appear unflappable on the surface, deep inside her there may be a lot of angst and unhappiness. She may carry the burden of complexes of being lesser than others and might feel insecure by the thought that she is not contributing to the household in a professional capacity.

On the other hand for employed woman, being an employee and a co-worker may increase her contact with people who can provide social support, as well as opportunities that may enhance her self esteem and sense of control. Hence, the differences between working women and housewives may be linked to generally higher levels of competence and self esteem among the working women, to greater feelings of social isolation among housewives, and to the greater opportunities for independence and self determination presented to women who work outside home.

The comparatively poor overall adjustment in educated housewives may be attributed to their perception that housework is more routine and involves more contact with things and less with people than paid work does. Further we will look into the differences among the two groups in various domains of adjustment, *i.e.* home, health, social and emotional.

Home adjustment is basically a purposeful transactional process as the individual lives in his/her family setting, advances educationally, pursues vocations, engages in social relationships, matures emotionally and grows into both physically and mentally healthy adult. Consequently, it is inevitable that the quality of adjustment varies with time and situation. The effectiveness of adjustment is measured in terms of how well a person copes with the changing circumstances. The present results indicated working women to be better adjusted in home as compared to the housewives. On the contrary, Kapur (1970) reported working women to be less effective in managing household responsibility than housewives and hence less adjusted in home.

As for the health front, the employed women were found

to be more satisfactorily adjusted than the non-working women. These findings have been supported by Epstein (1986) who found employed women to be physically healthier than non-employed women. The association of women's employment with good physical health could be causal, because something about employment improves health, or it could be selective, because healthy women work outside the home whereas unhealthy women do not.

No significant difference was observed between working and non-working women on social as well as emotional adjustment. However, the descriptive interpretation of mean scores suggested average social and emotional adjustment of both working and non-working women. Social adjustment refers to a change in habitual conduct or behaviour that an individual makes in order to fit into the community in which he/she lives, whereas, emotional adjustment is a prerequisite for social adjustment. It has been found that emotionally well adjusted persons are quick to establish affectional relations with others. These findings suggested that inspite of adopting the task roles, the socio-emotional role of women still seems to dominate. The busy schedule of the working women does not interfere much in proper allocation of time for emotional attachments with the members of family in particular and society in general. The insignificant difference between the two groups on social and emotional adjustment has not been supported by Pandey (1996) who found significantly better emotional and social adjustment among the non-working group as compared to the working women.

The working women typically carry the double burden of work and household commitments hence it is speculated that their lives are more pressured, more hectic and conflict ridden, and consequently, less satisfying than the lives of full time housewives. As also reported by Saxena (1996) that working women feel less satisfied than women fulfilling the single role of a housewife. But on the contrary the present study revealed that the potential conflicts and dissatisfaction accruing to the "double role" appeared to be offset by "the satisfactions of a career, social participation and independence.

These results can be explained on following grounds which explore what it is, that leads the housewives to have poor perception of themselves and to be less satisfied with their lives in general:

1. The full time housewives' structural base is typically more fragile than is the working women. The former generally occupies only one major social role, that of a housewife while the latter generally occupies two major roles, home maker and worker. Thus, they have two major sources of gratification—their family and their work and if they find one of these roles unsatisfactory, they can frequently focus their concern on the other role. In contrast, if non working women find their family role unsatisfactory, they typically have no major alternative source of gratification.

2. It seems reasonable to assume that housewives, find their major instrumental role, housekeeping, as frustrating. The characteristics of housework that seem to bring the most dissatisfaction are the lack of standards of performance, lack of recognition, social isolation and lack of pay fragmentation and monotony (Ferree, 1976). Moreover, being a housewife does not require a great deal of skill, for virtually all women whether educated or not, seem to be capable of being at least moderately competent housewives.

3. The role of housewife is relatively unstructured and invisible. It is possible for the housewives' to put things off, to let things slide, in sum, to perform poorly. The lack of structure and visibility allows them to brood over their troubles, and their distress may thus feed upon itself. In contrast, the women holding jobs must consistently and satisfactorily meet demands that constantly force them to be involved with their environment. Being forced to meet these structured demands, helps to draw their attention from their troubles and prevent them from being obsessed with worries. Besides this, the availability of social networks at work may help the working women to buffer the impact of stress in their lives, an advantage not shared by the housewives. **Infact status and resources are tied to employment role.** Women's employment decreases

economic hardship. It also brings satisfaction for women's several needs, more specifically for higher order needs such as self esteem and self actualization. This further explains for the better general health and quality of life among employed women.

4. Although relative to the paid work, housework provides more autonomy, as measured by the opportunity to decide both what work to do and how to do it (Bird and Ross, 1993). But the possibilities for autonomy vary—the freedom to set one's own schedule is limited when tasks are time dependent *e.g.* preparing meals. The repetitive nature of most domestic work reduces the housewife's ability to exercise autonomy because, once housewives impose a structure on their own work, that structure takes on a life of its own (Oakley, 1974). Rosenberg (1984) asserted that the autonomy of housework involves 'pseudo choices' among consumer goods, but no real decision making power or control over the working condition.

5. Housewives who are not employed are much more likely to feel that others are making **demands on them which leads to low levels of actual or perceived satisfaction with their lives.**

Both the working women and housewives experience rewards and costs for their roles in respective lives. Housewives may receive support from their spouse and family due to role conformity, but may feel lack of approval from significant others (Thakur and Misra, 1999) whereas the "can do" feeling in working women *i.e.* their sense of control and confidence in managing job and household chores, leads to self efficacy based self esteem. High self esteem in turn promotes positive affect ("feels" good about oneself) by buffering them against stress and other negative emotions, by enhancing personal adjustment coping and by promoting physical health (Baumeister, 1993). Employment hence seems to generate such resources for women which are so precious for them, that the investments involved are relatively less than what they reap. It appears that these resources are greater than the threat, and a desirable condition of surplus resources is brought about begetting something like 'eu-stress', a sense of control and positive association with the environment. Therefore, despite the strain of carrying a double role, the women with full time outside jobs are happier and feel themselves to be better off than the full time housewives. In short, the net effect of employment on an average emerges to be beneficial.

Next, the psychological status of women was studied in light of their professions and social roles they occupy. Regarding the **role conflict**, the present research addressed itself to answer following empirical questions :

1. How do the occupational differences affect the experience of role conflict in women.
2. In what major social role area, the conflict experienced by women is maximum.

The importance of quality of job has been highlighted by the present findings. Results revealed that women's experience of role conflict varied in large part with the social (familial) roles and occupational status.

Occupation is a characteristic that may influence the stressors to which people are exposed; those with higher occupational status often experience different stressful circumstances from those with lesser status jobs. Even when exposures to stressors are similar for the two, outcomes may well be conditioned by the occupational status. This is exactly what is seen in the present study. Despite of more work overload the doctors experienced moderate role conflict, whereas lecturers experienced least role conflict and the nurses were found to experience maximum role conflict at all levels of social roles.

Moreover, nurses who were married and having children experienced maximum role conflict than any other combination. No significant difference was however observed among the doctors holding different levels of social roles. This may be due to the fact that these distinct groups were stratified by occupational status. While the doctors were identified in high status group, the nurses fell in low status category.

Since the exposure to the role stressors cannot be predicted solely on the basis of role occupancy, the potential for stressful experience may lie in the conditions and demands of the role, as does the potential for rewards and gratification. Stress may result from the quality of experiences within and between roles and not from mere occupancy of roles (Barnett *et. al.* 1992). Having rewarding job and greater job control may offset the effects of more family responsibilities, especially against distress associated with children. Positive condition in one sphere of life may compensate for the negative conditions in another. In the present research too, the positive condition of gratification and control might have compensated for the negative condition of work overload in doctors whereas the high family demands combined with poor job situation may have led to more role conflict in nurses.

To elaborate it, the profession of doctors and lecturers provide more variety, autonomy, *i.e.* the freedom to make choices on the job, more control as compared to nurses whose job is more monotonous, expecting to follow and act according to the guidelines of the doctor with little control over the situation. 'Control' is the belief that one can exert some influence over the environment, either directly or indirectly, so that the environment becomes more rewarding and less threatening (Ganster and Fusilier, 1989). The stressfulness of task depends on the degree to which it can be controlled. **Job control, described as the beneficial ability to exert influence over one's work is especially valuable job characteristic for both male and female employee (Bond & Bruce, 2003).** If one's work role combines highly psychological demanding tasks with low level of control over the tasks, this combination exerts a major toll by simultaneously creating arousal and frustration. Therefore, although both—a **doctor** and a nurse being health care professionals may face similar levels of demands, still they may differ greatly in their power to control how to deal with these.

The high status jobs provides additional benefit of higher income which facilitates the ability to have extra paid help and support. Moreover, being independent wage earner one can use appropriate time saving devices or effort to hire domestic help to reduce one's time and labour inputs on household work (Mukhopadhayay, 1996). This enables these professionals, especially the married to get out of their houses with a free mind and in turn give them opportunity to realize and express themselves with fewer tensions of home management and child care. By and large the nurses reported having less hired help than the other two groups. As in nurses both their family and work require giving care and attention to the needs of others so, the increased responsibilities might have impeded the reconciliation of work and family responsibilities and they appeared to juggle numerous roles with considerable difficulty and stress.

Minimum level of role conflict among lecturers can also be explained in light of nature of job—regular versus irregular duty hours. Time has become increasingly scarce and valued commodity. As the growing number of women maintain their employment during the years of marriage, child rearing, a greater proportion of labour force is wrestling with work family cross pressures. Women working irregular hours have more problems than those working regular hours (Hemlata and Surya Naryana, 1983). In both nurses and doctors the timings of duties are too erratic since they require them to do night shifts along with the call duties. These irregular working hours leave little time for their families. As also reported earlier by Kanter (1977) that time spent at work directly reduces the time available for non-work roles. On the other hand, job of college lecturers require fixed time to be spent. Therefore, little overload allows them comparatively more quality time to be spent in house hold duties. Perceived lack of time combined with the feeling of guilt of not meeting the occupational and family demands appeared to be a source of more role conflict in nurses and doctors as compared to the lecturers.

In general, role conflict was found to increase with the increase in number of roles. More role conflict in married professional women in the present study derives from the contradictory values underlying their roles. As professional women they are expected to be committed to their work "just like men" at the same time as they are normatively required to give priority to their family. Further, the position seems to complicate when the woman attains motherhood. It is known that as the roles increase, so do the responsibilities. On one hand, motherhood is seen as an ultimate culmination of all of the woman's needs and aspirations and grants her status and fulfillment. On the other hand, coping with the children along with the increased responsibilities of husband and self at work place makes her life a nerve shattering experience. She may have to face numerous problems in both areas of work and home which may be broadly categorized into: relationship with husband, care of children, management of household duties, relationship with colleagues and management of office work. High demands sometimes results in less ability to satisfy any responsibility fully and thus the feeling that her life is out of control. Constantly in tension she is unable to do her best—neither as a mother nor as a worker. As reported by Rosenfield (1989) employed mothers with most of the responsibility for housework and child care have a low sense of control that reflects their role overload. This situation comes about because women who are shifting their focus to public sphere are getting confusing messages about family life. A strong insistence on education, autonomy and independence is mixed with sentimental messages about the family life. Conditioned into a caring role, women find these ideals produce a conflict. To avoid this, the homemakers' role having the responsibility of raising children continues to dominate the lives of most women. Pleck's (1977) often cited notion of "asymmetrical permeable boundaries" may function as a partial explanation of these findings, *i.e.* demands of the family roles are permitted to intrude into the work setting for women. This intrusion by family into work has the potential to create conflict in women as the socially prescribed sex role norm of women as primary caretakers of the family may conflict with the job norms.

The needs of children are given priority over employment. Although women may be keen to develop a career, work takes a secondary role whereas before marriage or having children it would automatically have come first. Similarly, Barnett and Baruch (1985) suggested role of a mother to be a women's primary source of stress whether alone or in combination with the work and the marital roles. Thus, the women who are single, married and mothers have available progressively fewer degrees of freedom for reducing the stress caused by increasingly demanding work expectations.

In case of **self esteem**, the doctors had higher self esteem at first and third level of social roles whereas lecturers showed higher self esteem at married social role. On the whole, doctors who were married and having children had highest self esteem.

The profession of doctors involve much more complexity, responsibility and challenge than nurses and lecturers. It entails being in contact with patients with life threatening diseases and finding cure for them. Still the noble work of treating the ill as well as their status in society makes their job much more satisfying and enriching. On personal front, although family role is extremely demanding in time and energy, it is also a major source of satisfaction for women. Individuals are often esteemed solely by virtue of their possessing a wide repertoire of roles: Quite apart from their ability to reward their role partners with special resources, such individuals benefit from a sheer presumption of superiority. Thus, some of the strain arising from multiple roles may be converted into social prestige, thereby offering a certain amount of psychic compensation. In present study also holding more number of social roles might have led to the feeling of completeness in the doctors who were married and mothers. This contentment on both the fronts: work and family may explain for their higher self esteem. The effect of multiplicity of the roles in doctors therefore seems to be mediated by their high occupational status and positive effects of familial roles which boasted their self esteem due to more rewarding job and gratification. This in turn may have moderated the effect of work overload (as shown below) and explains for low role conflict among married doctors having children than other two groups of professionals holding same level of social role.

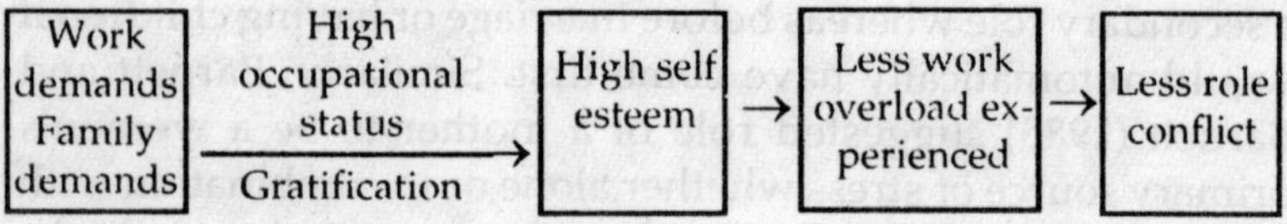

With regard to the overall **adjustment**, the lecturers among different professionals emerged as most satisfactorily adjusted. However, the social roles (main effects) did not have any significant effect. This may be explained in the light that women still accept the family role as their central role. Thus, to admit that they have problems within this role would undermine their sense of control and feminity. Therefore, women especially with more number of social roles may face dilemma with regard to their role expectation but even then they try endlessly to mould or adjust themselves to the existing situation.

At unmarried level, lecturers showed better overall adjustment, health adjustment and occupational adjustment. However, at the third level of social role doctors showed better overall adjustment, health adjustment as well as emotional adjustment. On the whole, the unmarried lecturers scoring low on different domains of adjustment showed more satisfactory adjustment (health, emotional, occupational). Comfortable nature of the work and less role conflict may have contributed to better adjustment of lecturers at their work place. Moreover, in the country like ours, unmarried women generally live with their parents or relatives which mean no major responsibility for them. Though they may be of great help in the home, still normally, they do not have binding with regard to the household management. Therefore, less responsibilities at home in addition to rather clear cut duties at work place provides the unmarried lecturers with enough room for themselves and their families and makes them better adjusted group. The satisfactory health adjustment in this group indicates the link between work load stress and physical health (Davidson and Cooper, 1983). Multiple role responsibilities and attendant role conflicts might have negatively affected health of women holding more number of social roles. Besides role conflict, age also seems to be an important contributor of health. With the advancing age the health status is found to deteriorate possibly explaining for the difference between unmarried and those who were married and mothers in this respect.

While comparing working and non-working women in the initial phase of study the former emerged as more satisfactorily adjusted group but the in depth study of social roles of working women revealed that the impact of employment on adjustment is not simply a matter of whether or not a woman is working outside the home but rather the extent to which that behaviour violates role expectations and creates role conflict.

Further, the **quality of life** of these women in four different domains was studied in relation to their professions. The facets in physical QOL domain explore the unpleasant physical sensations like aches, short-term pains experienced by a person, and the extent to which these sensations are distressing, person's dependence on medication. It also explore the energy, enthusiasm and endurance and working capacity that a person has in order to perform necessary tasks of daily living, and sleeping problems if any. In present research, unmarried lecturers were found to have better perception towards their health whereas married nurses having children were found to be lowest on this domain. The psychosomatic illnesses are profound consequences of the job stress experienced by nursing personnels across different public hospitals (Chandrasekar *et al.,* 1995). This could be due to the fact that, the nature of work demands them to work in standing position while attending to their medical and nursing needs. Secondly, they may have to run from place to place inside the hospital, very often, in order to support the doctors in their work. In addition, they may have to tolerate the administrative pressures, work overload etc.

The demand control model/role strain model presented by Karasek (1979) seems relevant at this point. This model suggests that job stress is a function of two structural characteristics: demands and control. It suggests that the work stress is determined by interactive effects of demand and control. First prediction of this model is that when psychological demands of job are high and worker's control over the task is low, then the most adverse reactions of psychological strain occurs (fatigue, anxiety, depression). Second prediction of the model involves the "active" and "passive" job categories. Increased motivation occurs in job situations where psychological demands are high and control is also high. Thus, while doctors would be considered to be in the active job, nurses would fall within the quadrant of high strain job. The working conditions of nurses combined with high demands and low control, results in imbalance between level of demand and control. As a consequence of this, ill health results. These findings also suggest that women in high status jobs may have better personal and coping resources at their disposal to deal with the role stressors.

One negative consequence of being able to make decisions about the work as in high status jobs is the likelihood of being held responsible or accountable when things do not work out as planned which may lead to anxiety. Other potential mitigators of the beneficial effects of control are the demands and time pressures that often accompany exercising control at work. Comparatively poor psychological quality of life among unmarried doctors may be because of the fact that a lot of responsibility is attached to their profession due to which they may sometimes experience negative feelings about the future or worry about the possible misfortunes.

Social relationships : the third domain of QOL examined the extent to which people feel the companionship, love and support they desire from the intimate relationship(s) in their life. It also examined how much a person feels the commitment, approval and availability of practical assistance from family and friends in sharing the responsibility and work together to solve personal and family problems. Results revealed the insignificant effects of professions and the social roles. Simply stating, irrespective of the professions, working women in the present study were satisfied with the kind of support they got from family and friends and with the extent of being able to express and fulfil their sexual desires. Women may be satisfied with the amount of help they received from their husbands because of their traditional thinking that household responsibilities were for wives. Allen and Hawkins (1999) put forth the concept of 'maternal gate keeping', a process in which wives limit their husbands' contributions to family work by setting, up rigid standards, controlling information, or actively discouraging their husbands' participation. Many women change their life styles to their husbands' choice rather than expect additional support from them.

The significant interactive effect of professions and social roles however suggested married doctors and lecturers to perceive more steady social ties, intimate and primary relationships. Unmarried professionals, though not necessarily socially isolated may have less access to such experiences. Marriage brings intimacy and may help create a stabilizing sense of security, belongingness and direction and provides a well defined social role because of which they may be more socially integrated.

The environmental QOL examined the person's sense of safety and security from physical harm, person's views of his/her financial resources and the extent to which these resources meet the needs for a healthy and comfortable life style. The focus was on what the person can afford or cannot afford might affect quality of life. It further examined the person's view of the health care in near vicinity, person's ability, opportunity and inclination to participate in leisure and pastimes, his/her view of how available or easy it is to find and use transport services to get around and freedom to perform chosen activities, etc. Married lecturers were found to have better perception in this regard indicating their general perspective on financial resources as "enough" to meet their needs. Moreover, being married provides additional economic benefits with married women having higher household income than the unmarried. As the profession of college lecturer involves spending comparatively less time on the job besides providing enough vacations throughout the year, they perceived enough opportunities for enjoyment of recreation and relaxation. The nature of their job *i.e.,* teaching also provides them enough opportunities for acquiring new information and skills.

Though people have strong belief about the positive effect of having and rearing children. Without them, women especially are said to feel empty. But the present findings indicated more towards the negative effect of being mothers in terms of poor perception of their lives (QOL) on the whole and poor general health.

The question then arises how could the children be loved and still increase the distress levels of mothers. It may be because children increase the economic hardships on families and also decrease the amount of emotional support that spouses receive from each other. The emotional well being and social support reduces the detrimental impact of children on health and quality of life of parents, especially mothers, but children seem to deplete these very resources. At the same level of family income, a family with children feels more economic pressures than the one without children. Moreover, children decrease the quality of marriage and the amount of support spouses get from each other, more specifically in women.

Besides this, during the role juggling episodes, mothers attempt to simultaneously meet the different objectives or to satisfy different demands but the satisfaction with the ability to do so may have been low and thus the negative consequences of managing so many roles might have stemmed in part from reduced control over events and outcomes. The role juggling effects may be compounded with work overload and the distress may have resulted not from simultaneous activity but from the fact that they actually had more to do during role juggling.

Through the present research the debate about whether multiple roles protect against distress and enhance QOL (role expansion hypothesis) or create overload and stress has given way to a recognition that the relationship between multiple social roles and QOL is mediated by a variety of factors like occupational status, income, number of children at home, age of children, type of family, help available, etc.

Considering the rising level of educational attainment by women, their involvement in paid employment is here to stay. Both freedom and strain are inextricably mixed in both family and job. On the basis of present research it can be summarized that it is not merely the occupancy of roles but the qualitative aspects of paid employment, marriage, motherhood and home making which may be associated with positive or negative outcomes. As also reported earlier by Belle in 1982 that although being employed is beneficial even to women in low level jobs but the advantages of employment are greater for women in occupation with higher status. Not all jobs are good for women-neither all the marriages, nor all the parenting experiences. It is the degree of "role burden" i.e. the feelings of involvement and responsibility as well as the role satisfaction, that affects the women's psychological state.

Intervention Strategies

Women have marked their existence by bringing out their own identity. Present work is a modest contribution in this area by exploring how women are psychologically responding to this double burden life style. An understanding of the relationship between social role occupancy and their respective psychological effects is essentially important since the configuration of roles that women adopts is not rigidly determined as for men.

The findings contribute to the current knowledge concerning professions, and social roles in relation to their psychological impact on working women and calls for immediate attention from the society in general and working women themselves in particular.

The findings suggest the desirability of efforts to design effective interventions to deal with family as well as work place strains. It instigates need to develop social policies at organisational and national level.

Intervention strategies with focus on individual and organization can be employed at primary, secondary and tertiary levels to bring out the best in working women.

At the primary level, the strategies aimed at individual may include **changes in life style of women** by inculcating appropriate leisure time, indulging in hobbies, improvement in time management, etc. to avoid stress. As noted by Pearlin (1983) it is around daily and enduring roles such as bread winning and work or marriage and parenthood that much of our lives are structured through time. Time is at a premium for every working woman, as she is always rushing against time. Therefore, a clear cut concept of time management taught to the working women can go a long way in making their lives easier.

Awareness programmes may be arranged to make the families aware of how women are important to the society and family and hence promoting support to working women. Expression of "importance" by family members may provide self pride to working women. The research underlies the need for sensitivity on the part of family members especially husbands. The family members may also be made aware that child rearing is not the sole responsibility of mothers. Meshing of work and family roles can produce strain so the couple as a unit may negotiate an optimal allocation of roles in order to reduce the pressure endemic to their situation. Proper sharing of household and child rearing responsibilities and sturdy support may enable them to contribute fruitfully and more effectively at home and work place.

At the organizational level approaches may be aimed at **restructuring the environment** to reduce the stress producing factors. Management may be persuaded to improve work design, work schedule and physical working environment; promote employees' career development and provide social support. Since the child care responsibilities are one of the important barriers that confront working women and are also found in present research to increase their role conflict and decrease their QOL therefore at the broader level, the present study suggests child care facilities of good quality to be provided at several locations.

At the secondary level focus on individual may include

training the women in proper stress response technique like relaxation, meditation, biofeedback, physical exercises, yoga, etc. The task of public policy should be to foster individual skills so that combining job and family roles becomes easier and more satisfying. Organisation may conduct regular **stress audit sessions** to gauge the level and cause of stress and further plan remedial actions.

At the tertiary level efforts may be symptom directed. When women cannot coordinate their several roles, stresses may arise and may harm their physical and mental well being. The adversely affected areas hereby detected in the present study can be improved by the **individual counselling** specifically aimed at reducing the stress in working women. At the organisational level efforts may be geared to rehabilitate stressed women by providing **social support at work** and extending expert help.

There is no denying of the fact that women are assets to the family and nation. In the words of Mahatma Gandhi, "As long as women of India do not take part in public life there can be no salvation for the country". Recent trends indicate an upswing in the employment rate among the women and so do the burden due to multiple roles in case of the wife and mother which seems crushing. Therefore, these strategies if taken into account can really help in creating a stress free healthy environment and hence allow these women to adjust more fully into their family and occupation.

Directions For Future Researches

The topic of present research is alive, explosive and controversial and needs a lot of attention and extensive studies. As the present study suffers from few limitations, the following redefinements and extensions of present problem may be undertaken :

1. As the results in the present research comprised of women in only three professions. Further researches are warranted of having true representative sample of women working in various other occupations.

2. Self efficacy may be an important dimension/parameter influencing the self esteem of a person. Therefore, further research might examine whether self efficacy acts as a mediator of multiple role juggling and its effect on adjustment, QOL etc.

3. Personality of the women might also influence their ability to juggle multiple roles as well as their coping skills. Research must be carried out in future to have an insight into the role of personality type (Type A/B, extraversion/introversion/neuroticism) in conjunction with role juggling.

4. The support available to the women from the spouse as well as the family members may moderate the negative outcomes emerging from handling number of social roles. So, future studies can focus on the link between social support and psychological effects of multiple role juggling.

5. Particular attention should be given to women's level of involvement in different roles as the effect would be greater for women who are high in both family and job demands.

6. Besides the self report inventories, some physiological measure like blood pressure, lipid protein, cortisol etc. is also recommended to strengthen the findings in regard to multiple role juggling.

7. Only the women in public sector were targeted in the present study. As there may be a lot of differences in the working conditions of public and private sectors. The researches drawing the comparison between women in these two different work setup may also be helpful.

8. Age range of working women was restricted to 45 years. But a lot of difference might exist between women having preschool children, college going children or independent children in influencing their coping

abilities with regard to multiple role juggling. The nature of role is found to change with age. Therefore, a comparatively large age range should be concentrated in the future researches.

9. It is suggested that the cognitive orientation of the working women if focussed with changing time frame, will certainly provide new insights in the area of multiple roles and their effects.

10. Although the present study is focused on working women, it is possible that similar effects would be found for other individuals facing multiple role demands. Future researches are therefore needed to determine the extent to which the present findings generalize to the other multiple role situations.

Exploring such issues will help to make an accurate assessment of the psychological impact of multiple roles. Moreover, with such directions for future studies, the results of these studies can provide a solid foundation for guiding corporate decision makers in designing job conditions and individuals in structuring a family life conductive to good quality of life.

REFERENCES

1. Abbot, D.A., & Brody, G.H. (1985). The Relation of Age, Gender and Number of Children to the Marital Adjustment of Wives. *Journal of Marriage and the Family, 47,* 77-84.

2. Aleshina, Y.Y., & Lektorskaya, Y.V. (1989). Role Conflict of a Working Women. *Veprosy Psikhologii,* Sep.-Oct. *(5),* 80-88.

3. Ali, J., & Avison, W.R. (1997). Employment Transitions and Psychological Distress : The Contrasting Experiences of Single and Married Mothers. *Journal of Health and Social Behaviour, 38,* 345-362.

4. Allen, S.M. & Hawkins, S.J. (1999). Maternal Gatekeeping : Mother's Beliefs and Behaviours That Inhibit Greater Father Involvement in Family Work. *Journal of Marriage and Family, 61,* 199-212.

5. Amatea, E.S., & Fong, M.L. (1991). The Impact of Role Stressors and Personal Resources on the Stress Experience of Professional Women. *Psychology of Women Quaterly, 15,* 419-430.

6. Aminabhavi, V.A., & Kulkarni, V.R. (2000). Mental Health of Working Women and Housewives. *Praachi Journal of Psycho-cultural Dimensions, 16 (1),* 33-35.

7. Aminah, A. (1996). Work-Family Conflict Among Married Professional Women in Malaysia. *Journal of Social Psychology, 136 (5),* 663-665.

8. Aneshensel, C.S. (1986). Marital and Employment Role Strain, Social Support and Depression Among Adult Women. In S.E. Hobfoll (Ed.) *Stress, Social Support, and Women* (pp. 99-114). New York : Hemisphere.

9. Aneshensel, C.S., & Pearlin, L.L. (1987). Structural Contexts of Sex Differences in Stress. In R.C. Barnett, Biener and G.K. Baruch (Eds.) *Gender and Stress.* New York : Free Press.

10. Aryee, S. (1992). Antecedents and Outcomes of Work-Family

Conflict Among Married Professional Women : Evidence from Singapore. *Human Relations, 45,* 813-837.

11. Aston, J., & Lavery, J. (1993). The Health of Women in Paid Employment : Effects of Quality of Work Role, Social Support and Cynicism on Psychological and Physical Well Being. *Women and Health, 20 (3),* 1—25.

12. Asuncion, L.M., Acevedo, M. Lopez, E.K., & Fernadez, M. (1993). Emotional Adjustment and Stress Associated with Sex Roles in Working and Non-Working Mothers. *Salud-Mental, 16 (2),* 13-23.

13. Bahr, S. & Day, R.D. (1976). *Sex Role Attitudes, Female Employment, and Marital Satisfaction.* Paper presented at the Annual Meeting to the National Council on Family Relations, New York.

14. Bandura, A. (1986). *Social Foundations of Thoughts and Action : A Social Congnitive Theory.* Englewood Cliffs, N.J. : Prentice-Hall.

15. Bandura, A. (1991). Self Regulation of Motivation Through Anticipatory and Self Regulatory Mechanisms. In R.A. Dienstbier (Ed.), *Perspective on Motivation : Nebraska Symposium on Motivation* (*38,* pp. 69-164). Lincoln : University of Nebraska Press.

16. Banton, M. (1965). In Fernandez, R. (1977). *The I, the Me and You—An Introduction to Social Psychology.* New York : Praeger.

17. Bardwick, J. (1971). *Psychological of Women : A Study of Bio-Cultural Conflicts.* New York : Harper & Row.

18. Barker, K. (1993). Changing Assumptions and Contingent Solutions : The Costs and Benefits of Women Working Full and Part Time. *Sex Roles, 28* (1—2), 47—71.

19. Barnett, R.C., & Baruch, G.K. (1985). Women's Involvements in Multiple Roles and Psychological Distress. *Journal of Personality and Social Psychology, 49,* 135-145.

20. Barnett, R.C., & Baruch, G.K. (1987). Social Roles, Gender, and Psychological Distress. In R. Barnett, L. Biener and G. Baruch (Eds.), *Gender and Stress.* New York : Free Press.

21. Barnett, R.C., Marshall, N.L., & Singer, J.D. (1992). Job Experiences Over Time, Multiple Roles, and Women's Mental Health : A Longitudinal Study. *Journal of Personality and Society Psychology, 62*, 634-644.

22. Barnett, R.C. (1993). Multiple Roles, Gender and Psychological Distress. In L. Goldberger and S. Breznitz (Eds.), *Handbook of Stress : Theoretical and Clinical Aspects* (Pp. 427-445). New York : The Free Press.

23. Baruch, G.K., Barnett, R.C., & Rivers, C. (1985). *Life Prints : New Patterns of Love and Work for Today's Women.* New York : Signet.

24. Baruch, G.K., Biener, L., & Barnett, R.C. (1987). Women and Gender in Research on Work and Family Stress. *American Psychologist, 42*, 130—136.

25. Baumeister, R.F. (1993). *Self Esteem. The Puzzle of Low Self Regard.* New York : Plenum.

26. Bedeian, A., Burke, G., & Moffett, R. (1988). Outcomes of Work-Family Conflict Among Married Male and Female Professionals. *Journal of Management, 14*, 475-491.

27. Beehr, T.A., & McGrath, J.E. (1992). Social Support, Occupational Stress and Anxiety. *Anxiety, Stress and Coping, 5*, 7-19.

28. Bell, H.M. (1961). *Manual for the Adjustment Inventory, Adult Form.* Stanford California : Consulting Psychologists.

29. Belle, D. (1982). Ed. *Lives in Stress : Women and Depression.* New Delhi : Sage.

30. Bernard , J. (1972). The Future of Marriage. New York : World Books.

31. Bhatty, I., & Bhatty, Z. (1971). Demographic Portrait of Professional Women Employed in Indian. In *Educated Women in Indian Society Today.* Bombay : Tata McGraw Hill.

32. Biddle, B.J., & Thomas, E.J. (ed.) (1996). *Role Theory : Concept and Research.* New York : Wiley.

33. Bird, C., & Fremont, A. (1989). Gender, Social Roles, and Health. Paper presented at the Annual Meeting of the American Sociological Association, San Francisco.

34. Bird, C.E., & Catherine, E.R. (1993). Houseworkers and Paid Workers : Qualities of Work and Effects on Personal Control. *Journal of Marriage and the Family, 55,* 913-925.

35. Birdsall, N. (1976). Women and Population Studies. *Journal of Women in Culture and Society, 1,* 699-712.

36. Bohen, H., & Viveros, L.A. (1981). *Balancing Jobs and Family Life : Do Flexible Schedules Really Help*? Philadelphia : Temple University Press.

37. Brenner, S.O., & Levi, L. (1987). Long Term Unemployment Among Women in Sweden. *Social Science and Medicine, 25,* 153-161.

38. Brief, A.P., & Hollenback, J.R. (1985). Work and the Quality of Life. Special Issue : Job Satisfaction. *International Journal of Psychology, 20(2),* 199-206.

39. Brody, E.M. (1985). Parent Care as a Normative Family Stress. *The Gerontologist, 25,* 19—29.

40. Broota, K.L. (1999). *Experimental Design in Behavioural Research.* New Delhi : New Age International.

41. Brown, G.W., Bhrolchain, M.N., & Harris, T. (1975). Social Class and Psychiatric Disturbance Among Women in an Urban Population. *Sociology, 9,* 225-254.

42. Burke, R., & Weir, T. (1976). Relationship of Wife's Employment Status to Husband-Wife and Pair Satisfaction. *Journal of Marriage and Family, 38,* 279-287.

43. Burke, R.J., & Greenglass, E.R. (1987). Work and Family. In : C. Cooper and I. Robertson (Eds.), *International Review of Industrial and Organizational Psychology.* (pp. 273-320). New York : Wiley.

44. Burke, R.J., & McKeen, C.A. (1995). Work and Career Experiences and Emotional Well Being of Managerial and Professional Women. *Stress Medicine, 11 (1),* 51-60.

45. Calhoun, L.G., Cheney, T., & Dawes, A.S. (1974). Locus of Control. Self Reported Depression, and Perceived Causes of Depression. *Journal of Consulting Psychology, 42,* 736-745.

46. Caltabiano, M.L., & Caltabiano, N.J. (1994). Prevalence of Type E multiple Role Stress in Professional Women and Impact of

Social Support in Affecting General Health. *Australian Journal of Marriage and Family, 15 (3),* 161-179.

47. Campbell, A., Converse, R. & Rodgers, W. (1970). *The Quality of American Life.* New York : Russel Sage.

48. Chakraborty, K. (1977). Some Variables in Role Conflict Analysis—the Case of Middle Class Working Mothers. *Sociologia Indica, 1 (1-2),* 37-47.

49. Chandrasekhar, S.F., Chandramauli, D., & Anjaiah, P. (1995), Job Stress and Psychosomatic Problems of Nurses at Select Hospitals. *Indian Journal of Applied Psychology, 32 (1-2),* 1-5.

50. Chattopadhyay, I., & Dasgupta, S.K. (1999). Good News About Role Stress(s). *Journal of the Indian Academy of Applied Psychology, 25 (1-2),* 35-38.

51. Chaudhury, S.M. (April 5, 2000). Money Cannot Buy Me Peace. *Delhi Times, The Times of India.*

52. Clausen, J.A. (1972). The Life Course of Individuals. In M.W. Riley, M. Johnson, and A. Foner (Eds.), *Aging and Society : A Sociology of Age Stratification.* (pp. 457-514). New York : Russell Sage Foundation.

53. Cleary, P., & Mechanic, D. (1983). Sex Differences in Psychological Distress Among Married People. *Journal of Health and Social Behaviour, 24,* 111-121.

54. Coit & Harper (1930). In Hemlata, P. & Suryanarayana (1983). Married Working Women : A Study on their Role Interactions. *Indian Journal of Social Work, XLIV (2),* 153-157.

55. Coleman, L.M., & Antonucci, T.C. (1983). Impact of Work on Women at Midlife. *Developmental Psychology, 19,* 290-294.

56. Cooke, R.A., & Rousseau, D.M. (1984). Stress and Strain from Family Roles and Work-Role Expectations. *Journal of Applied Psychology, 69,* 252-260.

57. Cooper, C.L., & Marshall, J. (1976). Occupational Sources of Stress : A Review of Literature Relating to Coronary Heart Disease and Mental Ill Health. *Journal of Occupational Psychology, 49,* 11-28.

58. Coopersmith, S. (1981). *Self Esteem Inventories.* California: Consulting Psychologists.

59. Coser, L. (1974). *Greedy Institutions.* New York : Free Press.

60. Coser, R., & Rokoff, G. (1971). Women in the Occupational World : Social Disruption and Conflict. *Social Problems, 18,* 535-554.

61. Cottrell, L.S., Jr. (1942). The Adjustment of the Individual to his Age and Sex Roles. *American Sociological Review, 4,* 617-620.

62. Cutrona, C.E. (1982). Transition to College : Loneliness and the Process of Social Adjustment. In L.A. Peplau & D. Pearlman (Eds.) *Loneliness: A Source Book of Current Theory, Research and Therapy* (pp. 291-309). New York : Wiley.

63. Cutter, S. (1986). Measuring the Quality of Life. *Futurist, 20,* 58-59.

64. Dahlstrom, E. (1967). *The Changing Roles of Men and Women.* London : Gerald Dickworth.

65. Davidson, M., & Cooper C. (1983). *Stress and the Woman Manager.* Oxford : Martin Robertson.

66. Deter, K.M. Feinleib, M., Mathews, K.A., & Kerr, B.W. (1987). The Federal Women's Study. In E.D. Eaker, B. Packard, N.K. Wenger, T.B. Clarkson, and H.A. Tyroler (Eds.), Coronary Heart Disease in Women : *Proceedings of an N.I.H. Workshop* (pp. 78-82). New York : Haymarket Doyma.

67. Devi, K., & Kumari, S. (1997). Relationship Between Socio-Economic Condition and Life Satisfaction of Hospital Staff (nurse). *Indian Psychological Review, 48 (2),* 101-104.

68. Eichler, A., & Parson, D.L. (Eds.) (1987). *Women's Mental Health : Agenda for Research.* Rockville, MD : National Institute of Mental Health.

69. Emmons, C.A., Biernat, M., Tiedje, L.B., Lange, E., & Wortman, C.B. (1990). Stress Support, and Coping Among Women Professionals with Preschool Children. In J. Eckenrode and S. Gore (Eds.), *Stress Between Work and Family* (pp. 61-93). New York : Plenum.

70. Epstien, C. (1983). The New Total Woman. *Working Woman,* April, 100-103.

71. Etzion, D., & Bailyn, L. (1994). Patterns of Adjustment to the Career/Family Conflict of Technically Trained Women in United States and Israel. *Journal of Applied Social Psychology, 24 (17),* 1520—1549.

72. Everly, G.S. (Jr.) (1989). *A Clinical Guide to the Treatment of Human Stress Response.* New York : Plenum.

73. Farmer, H.S. (1971). Helping Women to Resolve the Home Career Conflict. *Personnel and Guidance Journal,* 49, 795-801.

74. Ferree, M. (1976). The Confused American Housewife. *Psychology Today,* 76-80.

75. Frone, M.R., Russell, M., & Cooper, M.L. (1992). Antecedents and Outcomes of Work-Family Conflict : Testing a Model of Work-Family Interface. *Journal of Applied Psychology,* 77, 65, 78.

76. Ganster, D.C., & Fusilier, M.R. (1989). Control in the Work Place. In C.L. Cooper and I. Robertson (Eds.), *International Review of Industrial and Organizational Psychology* (pp. 235-280). London : Wiley.

77. Gerstel, N. Riessman, C.K., & Rosenfield, S. (1985). Examining the Symptomatology of Separated and Divorced Women and Men : The Role of Material Conditions and Social Networks. *Social Forces, 64,* 84-101.

78. Getzel, J.W., & Guba, E.G. (1954), Role, Role Conflict and Effectiveness. *American Sociological Review, 19,* 164-175.

79. Gilbert, L.A. (1984). Comments on the Meaning of Work in Women's Lives. *Counseling Psychologists, 12,* 129-130.

80. Girdano. D., & Everly, G. (1986). *Controlling Stress and Tension.* (2nd ed.) Englewood Cliffs, NJ : Prentice-Hall.

81. Glenn, N. (1975). The Contribution of Marriage to the Psychological Well Being of Males & Females. *Journal of Marriage and the Family, 37 (Aug.),* 594-600.

82. Goode, G.J. (1960). A Theory of Role Strain. *American Sociological Review, 25,* 483-496.

83. Goodman, L.J. (1975). The Longevity and Mortality of American Physicians, 1969-1973. *Milbank Memorial Funds Quarterly, 53,* 353-375.

84. Gorden, F.E., & Hall, D.T. (1974). Self image and Stereotype of Feminity : Their Relationship to Women's Role Conflict and Coping. *Journal of Applied Psychology, 59 (2),* 241-243.

85. Gove, W.R., & Tudor, J.F. (1973). Adults Sex Roles and Mental Illness. *American Sociological Review, 78,* 812-821.

86. Gove, W.R., & Geerken, M.R. (1977). The Effect of Children and Employment on the Mental Health of Married Men and Women. *Social Forces, 56,* 66-76.

87. Gove, W.R. & Hughes, M. (1979). Possible Causes of the Apparent Sex Differences in Physical Health : An Empirical Investigation. *American Sociological Review, 44,* 126-146.

88. Gove, M.R., Hughes, M.M., & Style, C.B. (1983). Does Marriage have Positive Effect on the Psychological well being of the Individual? *Journal of Health and Social Behaviour, 24,* 122-131.

89. Gove, W.R. (1984). Gender Differences in Mental and Physical Illness : The Effect of Fixed Roles and Nurturant Roles. *Social Science and Medicine,* 19, 77-91.

90. Gove, W.R., & Zeiss, C. (1987). Multiple Roles and Happiness. In F.J. Crosby (Ed.) *Spouse, Parent, Worker : On Gender and Multiple Roles.* (pp. 125-137). New Haven, CT : Yale University Press.

91. Grace, C.R. (1972). Role Conflict and Teacher. London : Routledge and Kegan Paul.

92. Gray, E.B., Lovejoy, M.C., Piotrkowski, C.S., & Bond, J.T. (1990). Husband Supportiveness and the Well Being of Employed Mothers of Infants. *Families in Society, 71 (6),* 332-341.

93. Gray-Toft, P.A., & Anderson, J.G. (1981). Stress Among Hospital Nursing Staff : Its Causes and Effects. *Social Science and Medicine, 15,* 639-647.

94. Greenberg, J., Pyszezynski, T., & Solomon, S. (1986). The Causes and Consequences of a Need for Self Esteem : A Terror

Management Theory. In R.F. Baumeister (Ed.), *Public Self and Private Self* (pp. 189-207). New York : Springer-Verlag.

95. Greenberg, J., Solomon, S., Pyszezynski, T., Rosenblatt, A., Burling, J., Lyon, D., Simon, L. & Pinel, E. (1992). Why do People Need Self Esteem? Converging Evidence that Self Esteem Serves as Anxiety Buffering Function. *Journal of Personality and Social Psychology, 63,* 913-922.

96. Greenglass, E.R. (1991). Type A Behaviour, Career Aspirations, and Role Conflict in Professional Women. In M.J. Strube (ed.) (1991), *Type A Behaviour* (pp. 277-292). Newbury Park, CA : Sage.

97. Greenhaus, J.H., & Beutell, N.J. (1985). Sources of Conflict Between Work and Non Work Roles. *Academy of Management Review, 11,* 164-177.

98. Greenhaus, J.J., & Beutell, N.J. (1985). Sources of Conflict between Work and Family Roles. *Academy of Management Review, 10,* 76-83.

99. Gutek, B.A., Nakamura, C.Y., & Nieva, V. (1981). The Interdependence of Work and Family Roles. *Journal of Occupational Behaviour, 2,* 1-16.

100. Gutek, B.A., Repetti, R.L., & Silver, D. (1988). Non-work Roles and Stress at Work. In C.L. Cooper and R. Payne (Eds.), Causes, Coping and Consequences of Stress at Work (pp. 141-174). New York : Wiley.

101. Hall, D. (1972). A Model of Coping with Role conflict : The Role Behaviour of College Educated Women. *Administrative Science Quarterly, 17,* 471-489.

102. Hall, D.T., & Hall, F.S. (1982). Stress and Two Career Couple. In C.L. Cooper and R. Payne (Eds.), Current Concerns in Cccupational Stress (pp. 254-266). New York : Wiley.

103. Hattery, A. (2001). *Women, Work, and Family : Balancing and Weaving.* Thousand Oaks, CA : Sage Publications, Inc.

104. Hauenstein, L.S., Kasl, S.V., & Harburg, E. (1977). Work Status, Work satisfaction and Blood Pressure Among Married Black and White Women. *Psychology of Women Quarterly, 1,* 334-349.

105. Haw, M.A. (1982). Women, Work and Stress. *Journal of Health and Social Behaviour, 23,* 132-144.

106. Haworth, J.T., Jarman, M., & Lee, S. (1997). Positive Psychological States in the Daily Life of a Sample of Working Women. *Journal of Applied Social Psychology, 27(4),* 345-370.

107. Haynes, S.G., & Feinleib, M. (1980). Women, Work and Coronary Heart Disease: Prospective Findings from the Famingham Heart Study. *American Journal of Public Health, 70,* 133-141.

108. Helson, R., Elliot, T., & Leigh, J. (1990). Number and Quality of Roles: A Longitudinal Personality View. *Psychology of Women Quarterly, 14,* 83-101.

109. Hemlatha, P., & Suryanarayana, M. (1983). Married Working Women: A Study on their Role Interactions. *The Indian Journal of Social Work, IX(2),* 153-156.

110. Higgins, C.A, Duxbury, L.E., & Irving, R.H. (1992). Work-Family Conflict in the Dual-Career Family. *Organizational Behaviour and Human Decision Processes, 51,* 51-75.

111. Higgins, C.A., & Duxbury, L.E. (1992). Work-Family Conflict: A Comparison of Dual Career and Traditional Career Men. *Journal of Organizational Behaviour, 13,* 389-411.

112. Hirsch, B.J., & Rapkin, B.D. (1986). Multiple Roles, Social Networks, and Women's WellBeing. *Journal of Personality and Social Psychology, 51,* 1237-1247.

113. Hochschild, A. (1989). Second Shift : Working Parents and the Revolution in the Home. New York : Viking.

114. Holahan, C., & Gilbert, I. (1979). Conflict Between Major Life Roles: Women and Men in Dual Career Couples. *Human Relations, 32,* 451-467.

115. Holahan, C.J., & Moos, R.H. (1981). Social Support and Psychological Distress: A Longitudinal Analysis. *Journal of Abnormal Psychology, 90,* 365-370.

116. Holahan, C.K., & Gilbert, L.A. (1979). Interrole Conflict for Working Women : Careers Versus Jobs. *Journal of Applied Psychology, 64(1),* 86-90.

117. Hong, J. & Seltzer, M. M. (1995). The Psychological Consequences of Multiple Roles : The Non-normative Case. *Journal of Health and Social Behavior, 36,* 386-398.

118. House, J.S. (1981). Work Stress and Social Support. Reading, MA : Addison-Wesley.

119. House, J.S., Strecher, V., Metzner, H.L., & Robbins, C.A. (1986). Occupational Stress and Health Among Men and Women in the Tecumseh Community Health Study. *Journal of Health and Social Behaviour, 27,* 62-77.

120. Houseknecht, S.K., & Macke, A.S. (1981). Combining Marriage and Career : The Marital Adjustment of Professional Women. *Journal of Marriage and the Family, 43,* 651-661.

121. Hughes, M., & Gove, W.R. (1981). Living Alone, Social Integration, and Mental Health. *American Sociological Review, 87,* 48-74.

122. Hughes, M.E. (1998). Interacting Effects of Multiple Roles on Women's Health. *Journal of Health and Social Behaviour, 39(September),* 216-236.

123. Husain, A., & Sharma, T. (1994). Marital Adjustment and Its Correlates among Working—Non Working Women. *Journal of Personality and Clinical Studies, 10(1-2),* 71-75.

124. Ilyas, Q.S. (1990). Determinants of Perceived Role Conflicting Among Women in Bangladesh. *Sex Roles, 22(3-4),* 237-248.

125. James, W. (1892). Psychology : The Briefer Course. New York : Henry Holt.

126. Jennings, S., Mazaik, C., & McKinlay, S. (1984). Women and Work : An Investigation of the Association Between Health and Employment Status in Middle-Aged Women. *Social Science Medicine, 19,* 423-431.

127. Jones, A.P., & Butler, M.C. (1980). A Role Transition Approach to the Stresses of Organizationally and Induced Family Role Disruption. *Journal of Marriage and the Family, 42,* 367-376.

128. Jyoti, G., & Malhotra, S. (2001). Social Roles and General Well Being. Unpublished M.Phil Dissertation, M.D. University, Rohtak.

129. Kahn, R.L., & Quinn, R.P. (1970). Role Stress—A Framework for Analysis. In A. McLean (ed.) *Mental Health and Work Organizations.* (pp. 50-115). Chicago : Rand McNally.

130. Kahn, R.L., Wolfe, D.M., Quinn, R.P., Snoek, J.D., & Rosenthal, R.A. (1964). Organizational Stress : Studies in Role Conflict and Ambiguity. New York : Wiley.

131. Kahn, S.E., Long, B.C., & Peterson, C. (1989). Marital and Parental Status and Quality of Life of Female Clerical Workers. *Canadian Journal of Counselling, 23(2),* 174-183.

132. Kakar, S. (1978). The Inner World : A Psychoanalytic Study of Childhood and Society in India. Delhi : Oxford University Press.

133. Kanter, R.M. (1977). Work and Family in the United States : A critical Review and Agenda for Research and Policy. New York : Russell Sage Foundation.

134. Kapur, P. (1974). Changing Status of the Working Women in India. Delhi : Vikas Publishing House Pvt. Ltd.

135. Karasek, R.A. (1979). Job Demands, Job Decision Latitude and Mental Strain : Implications for job Redesign. *Administrative Science Quarterly, 24,* 285-308.

136. Karasek, R.W., Schwartz, J., & Theorell, T. (1982). Job Characteristics, Occupation, and Coronary Heart Disease. Cleveland, OH : National Institute of Occupational Safety and Health.

137. Kasl, S.V. (1978). Epidemiological Contributions of the Study of Work Distress. In C.L. Cooper and R. Payne (Eds.) *Causes, Coping and Consequences of Stress at Work* (pp. 3-48). New York : John Wiley and Sons.

138. Katz, D., & Kahn, R.L. (1978). The Social Psychology of Organisations (2nd Ed.). New York : Wiley.

139. Kearl, M.C., & Gordon, C. (1992). *Social Psychology.* Boston : Allen and Bacon.

140. Keith, R., & Schafer, R. (1980). Role Strain and Depression in Two Job Families. *Family Relations, 29,* 483-488.

141. Kessler, R.C., & McCrae, J.A. (1982). The Effects of Wives' Employment on the Mental Health of Married Men and Women. *American Sociological Review, 47,* 216-227.

142. Kibria, N., Barnett, R.C., Baruch, G.K., & Marshall, N.L. (1990). Home Making Role Quality and Psychological Well Being and Distress of Employed Women. *Sex Roles, 22(5-6),* 327-347.

143. Kohn, M.C., & Schooler, C. (1983). Work and Personality : An Inquiry into the Impact of Social Stratification. Norwood, NJ : Ablex.

144. Kopelman, R.E., Greenhaus, J.J., & Connoly, T.R. (1983). A Model of Work, Family, and Interrole Conflict : A Construct Validation study. *Organizational Behaviour and Human Performance, 32,* 198-215.

145. Kornhauser, A. (1965). Mental Health of the Industrial Worker (293-322). New York : Wiley.

146. Kumari, P., & Singh, A.P. (2000). Life Stress and Some Personality Variables : A Comparison of Working Women and Housewives. *Journal of the Indian Academy of Applied Psychology, 26(1-2),* 25-31.

147. LaCroix, A.Z., & Haynes, S.G. (1987). Gender Differences in the Health Effects of Work Place Roles. In R.C. Barnett, L. Biener, and G.K. Baruch (Eds.), *Gender and Stress* (pp. 96-121). New York : Free Press.

148. Lambert, S.J. (1990). Processes Linking Work and Family : A Critical Review and Research agenda. *Human Relations, 43,* 239-257.

149. LaRocco, J.M., House, J.S., & French, J.R.P. (1980). Social Support, Occupational Stress, and Health. *Journal of Health and Social Behaviour, 3,* 202-218.

150. Lazarus, R.S. (1976). Patterns of Adjustment (3rd ed.). New York : McGraw Hill.

151. Lazarus, R.S., & Cohen, J.B. (1977). Environmental Stress. In I. Altman and J.F. Wohlwill (Eds.) *Human Behaviour and the Environment : Current Theory and Research.* New York : Plenum.

152. Lennon, M.C. (1994). Women, Work and Well Being: The Importance of Work Conditions. *Journal of Health and Social Behaviour, 35,* 235-247.

153. Lennon, M.C., & Rosenfield, S. (1992). Women and Mental

Health : The Interaction of Job and Family Conditions. *Journal of Health and Social Behaviour, 33*(December), 316-327.

154. Lewis, R.A., & Spanier, G.B. (1979). Theorizing About the Quality and Stability of Marriage. In W.R. Burr, R. Hill, N.I.Nye, and I.L. Reiss (Eds.), *Contemporary Theories about the family* (vol.1, pp. 268-294). New York : The Free Press.

155. Lewis, S.N.D., & Cooper, C.L. (1987). Stress in Two Earners and Stage in the Life Cycle. *Journal of Occupational Psychology, 60,* 289-303.

156. Link, B., Lennon, M.C., & Dohrenwend, B.P. (1992). Socio Economic Status and Depression : The Role of Occupations Involving Direction, Control and Planning. Paper presented at the annual meeting of the American Sociological Association, Pittsburgh, Pennsylvania.

157. Linton, R. (1936). The Study of Man. New Yor k: Appleton-Century -Craft.

158. London, M., Crandall, R., & Seals, G.W. (1977). The Contribution of Job and Leisure Satisfaction to Quality of Life. *Journal of Applied Psychology, 62,* 328-334.

159. Lorech, K., Russell, J., & Rush, M. (1989). The Relationship Among Family Domain Variables and Work-Family Conflict for Men and Women. *Journal of Vocational Behaviour, 35,* 288-308.

160. Luecken, L.J., Suarez, E.C., Kuhn, C.M., & Barefoot, J.C. (1997). Stress in Employed Women : Impact of Marital Status and Children at Home on Neurohormone Output and Home Strain. *Psychosomatic Medicine, 59(4),* 352-359.

161. MacKay, R. (1973). Conceptions of Children and Models of Socialization. In Hans Peter Dreitzel (Ed.), *Recent Sociology No. 5 : Childhood and Socialization.* New York : McMillan.

162. Macke, A.S., Bohrnstedt, G.W., & Bernstein I.N. (1979). Housewives' Self Esteem and Their Husbands Success : The Myth of Vicarious Involvement. *Journal of Marriage and the Family, Feb.,* 51-57.

163. Mandler, G. (1984). Mind and Body : Psychology of Emotion and Stress. New York : Norton.

164. Marcus, A.C., & Seeman, T.E. (1981). Sex Differences in Health Status : A Re-examination of the Nurturant Role Hypothesis. *American Sociological Review, 46(1),* 119-123.

165. Marcus, A.C., & Seeman, T.E. (1981). Sex Differences in Reports of Illness and Disability : A Preliminary Test of the 'Fixed Role Obligations' Hypothesis. *Journal of Health and Social Behaviour, 22(2),* 174-182.

166. Marcus, A.C., Seeman, T.E., & Telesky, C.W. (1983). Sex Differences in Reports of Illness and Disability : A Further Test of the Fixed Role Hypothesis. *Social Science and Medicine, 17,* 993-1002.

167. Marks, S.R. (1977). Multiple Roles and Role Strain : Some Notes on Human Energy, Time and Commitment. *American Sociological Review, 46(1),* 119-123.

168. Marshall, J., & Cooper, C.L. (1979). Executive Under Pressure : A psychological Study. London : MacMillan.

169. Martire, L. M., Stephens, M. A. P., & Townsend, A. L. (2000). Centrality of Women's Multiple Roles : Beneficial and Detrimental Consequences of Psychological Wellbeing. *Psychology and Aging, 15,* 148-156.

170. McBurney, D.H. (1994). Research Methods (3rd Ed.). California : Brooks/Cole.

171. McLanahan, S., & Adams, J. (1987). Parenthood and Psychological Well Being. *Annual Review of Sociology,* 237-257.

172. Meleis, A.I., Norbeck, J.S., & Laffrey, S.C. (1989). Role Integration and Health Among Female Clerical Workers. *Research in Nursing and Health, 12(6),* 355-364.

173. Menaghan, E.G. (1989). Role Changes and Psychological Well Being : Variations in Effects by Gender and Role Repertoire. *Social Forces, 67,* 693-714.

174. Meon, P., McClain, D.D., & Williams, R.M. (1992). Successful Aging : A Life Course Perspective on Women's Multiple Roles and Health. *American Journal of Sociology, 97,* 1612-1638.

175. Merikangas, K. (1985). Sex Differences in Depression. Paper presented at the Murray Centre (Radcliffe College) Conference : *Mental Health in Social Content,* Cambridge.

176. Misra, P., & Bajpai, V. (1998). Role Conflict : The Spill Over Effects. *Journal of the Indian Academy of Applied Psychology, 24(1-2),* 27-31.

177. Moore, D., & Gobi, A. (1995). Role Conflict and Perceptions of Gender Roles : *The case of Israel. Sex Roles, 32(3-4),* 251-270.

178. Mostow, E., & Newberry, P. (1975). Work Role and Depression in Women : A Comparison of Workers and Housewives in Treatment. *American Journal of Orthopsychiatry, 45,* 538-548.

179. Mukherjee, R. (1980). On the Appraisal of Quality of Life. In A. Szalai, and F.M. Andrews (Eds.), *The Quality of Life : Comparative Studies.* Beverly Hills : Sage.

180. Mukhopadhyay, S. (1996). Anxiety Level and Its Temporal Change Among Working Mothers in Calcutta. *The Journal of Social Psychology, 136(1),* 123-125.

181. Napholz, L. (1995). Indexes of Psychological Well Being and Role Commitment Among Working Women. *Journal of Employment Counseling, 32(1),* 22-31.

182. Nathawat, S.S., & Mathur, A. (1993). Marital Adjustment and Subjective Well Being in Indian— Educated Housewives and Working Women. *Journal of Psychology, 127,* 353-358.

183. Nation, J.R. (1997). Research Methods. London : Prantice Hall International.

184. Nieva, V.F., & Gutek, B.A. (1981). Women and Work : A Psychological Perspective. New York : Praeger.

185. Noor, N.M. (1995). Work and Family Roles in Relation to Women's Well Being : A Longitudinal Study. *British Journal of Social Psychology, 34,* 87-106.

186. Noor, N.M. (1997). The Relationship Between Wives Estimates of Time spent Doing Housework, Support and Wives Well Being. *Journal of Community and Applied Social Psychology, 7(5),* 413-423.

187. Nordenmark, M. & Strandh, M. 1999. Towards a Sociological Understanding of Mental Well-being Among the Unemployed : The Role of Economic and Psychosocial Factors, *Sociology, 33 (3),* 577-97.

188. O'Driscoll, M., & Humphries, M. (1992). Time Demands, Interrole Conflict and Coping Strategies Among Managerial Women. Unpublished Paper, University of Waikato, Newzealand.

189. Oakley, A. (1974). The Sociology of Housework. New York : Pantheon.

190. Orden, S.R., & Bradburn, N.M. (1968). Working Wives and Marriage Happiness. *American Journal of Sociology, 74,* 392-407.

191. Ozer & Bandura (1990). In Ozer, E.M. (1995). Impact of Childcare Responsibility and Self Efficacy on the Psychological Health of Professional Working Mothers. *Psychology of Women Quarterly, 19,* 315-335.

192. Ozer, E.M. (1995). The Impact of Child Care Responsibility and Self Efficacy on the Psychological Health of Professional Working Mothers. *Psychology of Women Quarterly, 19(3),* 315-335.

193. Pandey, A.K. (1999). Manual for Role Conflict Scale. As Mentioned in the Catalogue. Agra : National Psychological Corporation.

194. Pandey, M. (1996). Professionalism Versus Socialism : A Study of Women Employment. *Indian Journal of Psychometry and Education, 27(2),* 77-80.

195. Pareek, A., & Mehta, M. (1997). Role Stress Among Working Women. In D.M. Pestonyee, & U. Pareek (Eds.), *Studies in Organizational Role Stress and Coping* (pp. 173-181). New Delhi : Nice.

196. Pareek, U. (1976). Inter-role exploration. In J.W. Pfeiffer and J.E. Jones (Eds.) The 1976 Annual Handbook for Group Facilitators (pp. 211-224). California : University Associates.

197. Parry, G. (1987). Sex Role Beliefs, Work Attitudes and Mental Health in Employed and Non-Employed Mothers. *British Journal of Social Psychology, 26,* 47-58.

198. Parson, T. (1951). The Social System. Glencoe, 111 : Free Press.

199. Parsons, T., & Bales, R.F. (1955). Family, Socialization and Interaction Process. New York : Free Press.

200. Paterson, L.R. (1978). An Exchange Analysis of Family Roles and Marital Satisfaction. *Diss. Abst. Int., 38(9),* 5746.

201. Pattison, H.M., & Moyse, K.I. (1995). The Effects of Suitability for Current Role on the Psychological Well Being of Employed and Non-Employed Mothers. *Journal of Reproductive and Infant Psychology, 13(3-4),* 229-236.

202. Payton, M., & Brayfield, A.H. (1976). The Good Job and Good Life : Relation of Characteristics of Employment to General Well Being. In A.D. Biderman and T.F. Drury (Eds.), Measuring Work Quality of Social Reporting (pp.125-150). New York : Sage.

203. Pearlin, L.I. (1975). Status in Equality and Stress in Marriage. *American Sociological Review, 40,* 344-357.

204. Pearlin, L.I. (1983). Role Strains and Personal Stress. In H.B. Kaplan (Ed.) Psychosocial Stress : Trends in Theory and Research (pp. 3-32). New York : Academic press.

205. Pearlin, L.I. (1989). The Sociological Study of Stress. *Journal of Health and Social Behaviour, 30,* 241-256.

206. Pearlin, L.I., & Johnson, J. (1977). Marital Status, Life Strains and Depression. *American Sociological Review, 42,* 704-715.

207. Pearlin, L.I., Lieberman, M.A., Menaghan, E.G., & Muller, J.J. (1981). The Stress Process. *Journal of Health and Social Behaviour, 22,* 337-356.

208. Pietromonaco, P.R., Manis, J., & Frohardt, L.K. (1984). Psychological Consequences of Multiple Social Roles. Paper Presented at the Meeting of the American Psychological Association, Toronto.

209. Pietromonaco, P.R., Manis, J., & Frohardt, L.K. (1986). Psychological Consequences of Multiple Social Roles. *Psychology of Women Quarterly, 10,* 373-381.

210. Pleck, J.H. (1977). The Work-Family Role System. *Social Problems, 24,* 417-427.

211. Pleck, J.H., Staines, G., & Lang, L. (1980). Conflict Between Work and Family Life. *Monthly Labour Review, 103,* 29-32.

212. Radloff, L. (1975). Sex Differences in Depression : The Effects of Occupation and Marital Status. *Sex Roles, 1,* 249-265.

213. Rani, G., & Yadav, A. (2000). Anxiety Level Among Working Women. *Journal of Personality and Clinical Studies, 16(1),* 63-67.

214. Rani, K. (1976). Role Conflict in Working Women. New Delhi : Chetan Publications.

215. Rankin, E.D. (1993). Stresses and Rewards Experienced by Employed Mothers. *Health Care for Women International, 14(6),* 527-537.

216. Rapoport, R., & Rapoport, R.N. (1978) (Eds.) Working Couples. London : Routledge & Kegan Paul.

217. Rapoport, R., & Rappport, R. (1971). Dual Career Families. Baltimore : Penguine.

218. Rauch, R.A. (1990). A quality of Life should be Full of Values. USA Today, Jan., 73-74.

219. Reifman, A., Biernat, M., & Lang, E.L. (1991). Stress, Social Support, and Health in Married Professional Women with Small Children. *Psychology of Women Quarterly, 15(3),* 431-445.

220. Repetti, R.L., Mattews, K.A., & Waldron, I. (1989). Employment and Women's Health : Effects of Paid Employment on Women's Mental and Physical Health. *American Psychologist, 44,* 1394-1401.

221. Reskin, B. & Padavic, I. (1994). *Women and Men at Work.* Thousand Oaks, CA : Pine Forge Press.

222. Rice, D.P., & Cugliani, A.S. (1979). Health Status of American Women. (72-78) in Proceedings of the American Statistical Association. Washington, D.C. : American Statistical Association.

223. Riesch, S.K. (1984). Occupational Commitment and Quality of Maternal—Infant Interaction. *Research in Nursing and Health, 7,* 295-303.

224. Rose, A.M. (1955). Factors Associated with the Life Satisfaction of Middle Aged Persons. *Marriage and Family Living, 17,* 15-19.

225. Rosenberg, M.J. (1965). When Dissonance Fails : On Eliminating Evaluation Apprehension from Attitude

Measurement. *Journal of Personality and Social Psychology, 1,* 28-42.

226. Rosenfield, S. (1989). The Effects of Women's Employment : Personal Control and Sex Differences in Mental Health. *Journal of Health and Social Behaviour 33,* 213-25.

227. Ross, C.E., & Mirowsky, J. (1988). Child Care and Emotional Adjustment to Wives' Employment. *Journal of Health and Social Behaviour, 29,* 127-138.

228. Ross, C.E., & Mirowsky, J. (1995). Does Employment Affect Health? *Journal of Health and Social Behaviour, 36,* 230-243.

229. Rout, U.R., Lewis, S., & Kagan, C. (1999). Work and Family Roles : Indian Cancer Women in India and the West. *Indian Journal of Gender Studies, 6(1),* 91-108.

230. Russo, N. (1976). The Motherhood Mandate. *Journal of Social Issues, 5,* 143-154.

231. Sargent, S.S. (1957). Conception of Role and Ego in Contemporary Psychology. In J. Rohrer and M. Sherif (Eds.) *Social Psychology at Crossroads.* New York : Harper.

232. Saxena, M.R. (1996). Life Satisfaction and Perceived Happiness as a Function of Family Structure and Employment of Women. *Indian Journal of Psychometry and Education, 27(1),* 41-46.

233. Schooler, C., Miller, J., Miller, K.A., & Ritchtand, C.N. (1984). Work for the Household : Its Nature and Consequences for Husband and Wives. *American Journal of Sociology, 90,* 97-124.

234. Secord, P.F., & Backman, C.W. (1964). *Social Psychology.* New York : McGraw Hill.

235. Sekaran, U. (1983). Factors Influencing Quality of Life in Dual Career Families. *Journal of Occupational Psychology, 56,* 161-174.

236. Sen, P.C. (1981). Personal and Organizational Correlates of Role Stress and Coping Strategies in Some Public Sector Banks. Unpublished Ph.D thesis in management, University of Gujarat, Ahmedabad.

237. Senecal, C., Vallerand, R. J. & Guay, F. (2001). Antecedents and Outcomes of Work-Family Conflict : Toward a

Motivational Model. *Personality and Social Psychology Bulletin, 27,* 176-186.

238. Shibutani, T. (1961). Society and Personality. Englewood Cliffs, N.J. : Prentice Hall.

239. Sieber, S.D. (1974). Toward a Theory of Role Accumulation. *American Sociological Review, 39,* 567-578.

240. Singh, A., & Bawa, S.K. (1996). Adjustment Problems of Working Women. *Praachi Journal of Psycho-Cultural Dimensions 12(1),* 15-20.

241. Singh, B. (1997). Anxiety Among Working and Non-Working Women. Praachi *Journal of Psycho-Cultural Dimensions, 13(2),* 105-108.

242. Singh, K.P. (1972). Career and Family—Women's Two Roles (A study in role conflict). *Indian Journal of Social Work XXXIII(3),* 227-281.

243. Sinha, P. (1981). Determinants of Role Conflict Among Female Teachers, Unpublished Doctoral Thesis, Patna University, Patna.

244. Sinha, P. (1986). Assessing Quality of Life. *Indian Psychological Review, 30,* 1-8.

245. Smith, D.S. (1985). Wife Employment and Marital Adjustment : A Cumulation of Results. *Family Relations, 34,* 483-490.

246. Sorensen, G., & Verbrugge, L.M. (1987). Women, Work and Health. *Annual Review of Public Health, 8,* 235-251.

247. Sound, K., & Ostwald, S.K. (1985). Dual Earner Families' Stress Levels and Personal and Life Style Related Variables. *Nursing Research, 34,* 357-361.

248. Spreitzer, E., Synder, E.E., & Larson, D.L. (1979). Multiple Roles and Psychological Well Being. *Sociological Focus, 12,* 141-148.

249. Stewart, A.S., & Salt, P. (1981). Life Stress, Lifestyles, Depression, and Illness in Adult Women. *Journal of Personality and Social Psychology, 40,* 1063-1069.

250. Steyn, A.F. (1997). Marital Integration in the Dual Career Family. In Dreman, Solly (Ed.), The Family on the Threshold

of the 21st Century : Trends and Implications (pp. 87-99). Mahwah, N.J. : Lawrence Erlbaum Associates.

251. Stryker, S. (1980). Symbolic Interactionism : A Social-Structural Version. Menlo Park, CA : Benjamin/Cummings.

252. Strykowska, M. (1991). Family and the Psychological Mechanism of Women's Occupational Functioning. *Przeglad Psychologiczny, 34(3),* 495-508.

253. Symonds, P.M. (1951). The Ego and the Self. New York : Appleton-Century-Crofts.

254. Szalai, A. (1972). The Use of Time : Daily Activities of Urban and Suburban Populations in Twelve Countries. The Hague : Mouton.

255. Szalai, A. (1980). The Meaning of Comparative Research on the Quality of Life. In A. Szalai and F.M. Andrews (Eds.), The Quality of Life : Comparative Studies (7-21). Beverly Hills : Sage.

256. Tedeschi & Norman (1985). In Leary, M.R., Tambor, E.S., Terdal, S.K. and Downs, D.L. (1995). Self Esteem as an Interpersonal Monitor : The Sociometer Hypothesis. *Journal of Personality and Social Psychology 68(3),* 518-530.

257. Terborg, J.R. (1977). Women in Management : A Research Review. *Journal of Applied Psychology, 62,* 647-664.

258. Thakar, G., & Misra, G. (1995). Role of Age and Type of Family in Coping with Daily Hassles Among Employed Women. Unpublished manuscript, Bhopal University, Bhopal.

259. Thoits, P.A. (1983). Multiple Identities and Psychological Well Being : A Reformulation and Test of the Social Isolation Hypothesis. *American Sociological Review, 48,* 174-187.

260. Thoits, P.A. (1992). Identity Structures and Osychological Well Being : Gender and Marital Status Comparisons. *Social Psychological Quaterly, 55,* 236-56.

261. Umberson, D. & Gove, W. R. (1989). Parenthood and Psychological Well-Being. *Journal of Family Issues, 10,* 440-462.

262. Van Meter, M.J.S., & Agronow, S.J. (1982). The Stress of Multiple Roles : The Case for Role Strain Among Married College Women. *Family Relations, 31,* 131-138.

263. Vanfossen, B.E. (1981). Sex Differences in the Mental Health Effects of Spouse Support anD equity. *Journal of Health and Social Behaviour, 22,* 130-143.

264. Verbrugge, L.M. & Madans, J.H. (1985). Social Roles and Health Trends of American Women. *Milbank Memorial Fund Quarterly/Health and Society, 63.*

265. Verbrugge, L.M. (1979). Marital Status and Health. *Journal of Marriage and the Family, 41,* 267-285.

266. Verbrugge, L.M. (1982). Women's Social Reoles and Health. In P. Berman and E. Ramey (Eds.), Women : A Developmental Perspective. Bethesda, *MD : National Institutes of Health.*

267. Verbrugge, L.M. (1983). Multiple Roles and Physical Health of Women and Men. *Journal of Health and Social Behaviour, 24,* 16-30.

268. Verbrugge, L.M. (1986). From Sneezes to Adieux : Stage of Health for American Men and Women. *Social Science and Medicine, 22,* 1195-1212.

269. Verbrugge, L.M. (1987). Role Responsibilities, Role Burdens and Physical Health. In F.J. Crosby (Ed.), Spouse, Parent, Worker : On Gender and Multiple Roles (pp. 154-66). New Haven, M.A : Yales University Press.

270. Vijayalaxmi, A.A., & Kulkarni, V.R. (2000). Mental Health of Working Women and Housewives. *Praachi Journal of Psycho-Cultural Dimensions, 16(1),* 33-35.

271. Voydanoff, P. (1988). Work Role Characteristics, Family Structure Demands, and Work-Family Conflict. *Journal of Marriage and the Family, 50,* 749-761.

272. Waldron, I. (1978). The Coronary-Prone Behaviour Pattern, Blood Pressure, Employment and Socio Economic Status in Women. *Journal of Psychosomatic Research, 22,* 79-87.

273. Waldron, I., & Herold, J. (1986). Employment, Attitude Towards Employment, and Women's Health. *Women and Health, 11,* 79-98.

274. Waldron, I., & Jacobs, J.A. (1989). Effects of Labour Force Participation on Women's Health—New Evidence from a Longitudinal Study. *Journal of Occupational Medicine, 30,* 977-983.

275. Waldron, I., & Jacobs, J.A. (1989). Effects of Multiple Roles on Women's Health—Evidence from a National Longitudinal Study. *Women and Health, 15,* 3-19.

276. Walker, L.O., & Best, M.A. (1991). Well Being of Mothers with Infant Children : A Preliminary Comparison of Employed Women and Homemakers. *Women and Health, 17(1),* 71-89.

277. Warr, P., & Parry, G. (1982). Paid Employment and Women's Psychological Well Being. *Psychological Bulletin, 91,* 498-516.

278. Wharton, A.S., & Erickson, R.J. (1995). The Consequences of Caring : Exploring the Links Between Women's Job and Family Emotion Work. *Sociological Quaterly, 36(2),* 273-296.

279. WHO QOL group (1996). Manual for WHO QOL—BREF : Field Trial Version. New Geneva, *World Health Organization.*

280. Williams, K.J., Suls, J., Alliger, G.M., & Learner, S.M. (1991). Multiple Role Juggling and Daily Mood States in Working Mothers : An Experience Sampling Study. *Journal of Applied Psychology, 76(5),* 664-674.

281. Winefield, A, Montgomery, B, Gault, U, Muller, J, O'Gorman, JH, Reser, J & Roland, D 2002, The Psychology of Work and Unemployment in Australia Today : An Australian Psychological Society Discussion Paper. *Australian Psychologist,37(1),* 1-9

282. Wirth, L. (1938). Urbanism as a Way of Life. *American Journal of Sociology, 44,* 8-20.

283. Wolman, B.B. (1973). The Dictionary of Behavioural Science.. New York : Van Nostrand Reinhold.

284. Woods, N.F. (1978). Women's Roles, Mental Ill Health and Illness Behaviour. Unpublished Doctoral Thesis, University of North Carolina, North Carolina.

285. Woods, N.F. (1985). Employment, Family Roles, and Mental Ill Health in Young Married Women. *Nursing Research, 34,* 4-10.

286. Woods, N.F., & Hulka, B.S. (1979). Symptom Reports and Illness Behaviour Among Employed Women and Homemakers. *Journal of Community Health, 5,* 36-45.

287. Wortman, C., Biernat, M., & Lange, E. (1991). Coping with Role Overload. In M. Frankenhaeuser, U. Lundberg and M. Chesney (Eds.) Women, Work and Health. New York : Plenum.

288. Wright, J.D. (1978). Are Working Women Really More Satisfied? Evidence from Several National Surveys. *Journal of Marriage and the Family, 40(May),* 301-313.

289. Yogev, S. (1981). Do Professional Women have Equalitarian Marital Relationship? *Journal of Marriage and the Family, 43,* 865-871.

290. Ziller, R. (1969). The Alienation Syndrome : A Triadic Pattern of Self—other Orientation. *Sociometry, 32,* 287-300.

INDEX